Also available in Red Fox
by Steve and Megumi Biddle

Amazing Origami For Children
Things To Make In The Holidays
Newspaper Magic
The Paint and Print Fun Book
Magical String
Amazing Flying Objects
Make Your Own Greetings Cards

About the authors

Steve Biddle is a professional entertainer and Origami expert. He has been teaching Origami to children and adults since 1976. While he was in Japan studying under the top Japanese Origami Masters, he met and married his wife Megumi. Megumi is one of the foremost Japanese paper artists working in *Washi* hand-made Japanese paper, and her work has received many top awards in Japan and abroad. She has designed for some of Japan's top fashion designers, and has worked on many award-winning commercials for Japanese television. Since their return to England, Steve and Megumi have taken their craft all over the country to schools, festivals and arts centres, and have designed for television and feature films. They present Origami as entertainment, art and education to young and old alike.

THE CHRISTMAS ORIGAMI BOOK

Steve and Megumi Biddle

Illustrations by Megumi Biddle

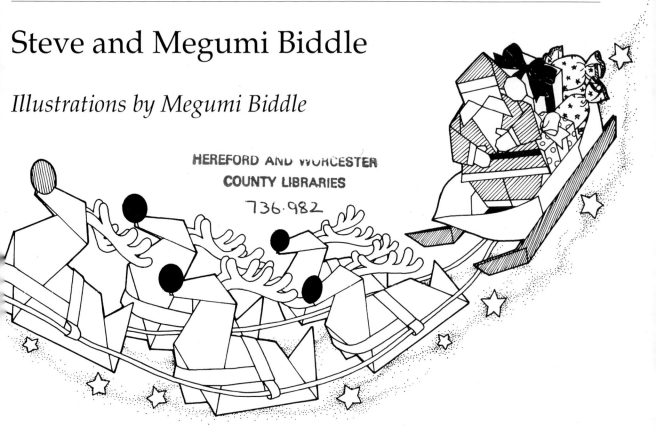

RED FOX

A Red Fox Book

Published by Random Century Children's Books
20 Vauxhall Bridge Road, London SW1V 2SA

A division of the Random Century Group

London Melbourne Sydney Auckland Johannesburg
and agencies throughout the world

First published by Red Fox 1992

Set in Adobe Palatino

Made and printed in Hong Kong

Contents

Introduction

The Christmas Origami Book is designed to help you and your family experience the holiday at its best. First you will find instructions to help you create beautiful and useful origami projects for the festive season. Decorate your tree with delightful origami ornaments, a three-dimensional star, and a snowman. Decorate your home with sprigs of origami holly and mistletoe, a jolly Father Christmas, and a variety of table and party decorations that are bursting with Christmas spirit.

Making decorations and giving gifts have become a very special part of the holiday. So beginning on page 86, you will find instructions on how to make your own Christmas crackers and garlands, along with tips on gift wrapping and packaging. They contain a wealth of ideas, brimming with originality and tradition.

Each Origami and Christmas craft project begins with a short list of materials you will need before you start. More often than not, all that you require is a pencil, ruler, scissors, glue, paper, needle and cotton and a few other everyday materials that can be found around the home, or bought from any good stationery shop for just a few pence. It is a good idea to keep all these materials together in a safe place, such as a box with a lid, and out of reach of any younger members of the family.

You may be wondering what sort of paper to use for the origami projects. Most of the models in this book are folded from a square of paper, although in a few cases you will need more than just one. All kinds of paper can be folded into origami, but do try to find a paper that suits you best. Packets of origami paper, coloured on one side and white on the other, can be obtained from

department stores, toy shops, stationery shops and oriental gift shops. Other papers suitable for origami can be found in art and craft shops. Why not try using the fancy gift wrapping papers that are now widely available? You could even cut out a few pages from a colour magazine! Your paper does not have to be coloured on one side, but it can help to make the finished origami look very attractive.

Do not panic if you have problems with your first few attempts. Check the illustration to see what has to be done. Look at the next illustration to see what shape your paper should make as the result of the step you are following. Also remember that the arrows show the direction in which the paper has to be folded. So look very carefully at the illustrations to see which way the arrows go over, through, and under, and fold your paper accordingly. To help you become accomplished at paper folding, here are some very helpful tips:

★ Fold on a flat surface, such as a table or a book.
★ Make your folds neat and accurate.
★ Crease your folds into place by running your thumb nail along them.
★ In the illustrations, the shading represents the coloured side of the paper.
★ Try to take great care in obtaining the right kind of paper to match the origami that you plan to fold. This will help enhance the finished product.
★ Before you start, make sure your paper is square.
★ Above all, if a fold or a whole model does not work out, do not give up hope. Put the fold to one side and come back to it another day.

Through our television series called *Origami with Steve and Megumi* and our many appearances at schools, libraries and art centres, we have chosen models that have been fun to show and share with others. Many of the models are traditional, some we have adapted and developed from traditional ones, while a few others have been especially created for *The Christmas Origami Book*.

If you want to learn more about origami, contact the British Origami Society, 11 Yarningale Road, Kings Heath, Birmingham, B14 6LT.

In the United States, contact the Friends of the Origami Centre of America, 15 West 77th Street, New York, NY 10024-5192.

If you do have trouble in finding 'snaps' for Christmas crackers, contact Lewis Davenport Ltd., 7 Charing Cross Underground Shopping Arcade, The Strand, London, WC2N 4HZ.

We would very much like to hear from you about your interest in origami, or if you have any problems obtaining origami materials. So please write to us, care of our publishers, enclosing a stamped addressed envelope.

We do hope that you have a great deal of fun and enjoyment with *The Christmas Origami Book*. Here's wishing you a Merry Christmas – and a very busy paper folding one!

Steve and Megumi

Acknowledgements

Our deepest thanks go to Joan Morrison and John Cunliffe for their help and support.

How to make a square

Many of the models to be found in *The Christmas Origami Book* start with a square of paper. So here is a quick and easy way to make one.

You will need:

Rectangle of paper, coloured on one side and white on the other
Scissors

1 Place the rectangle sideways on, with the white side on top. Fold the left-hand side . . .

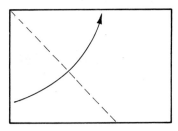

2 up to meet the top, so making . . .

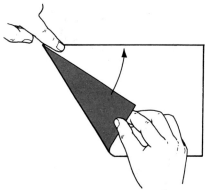

3 a triangle. Cut along the side of the triangle. Discard the rectangular piece of paper.

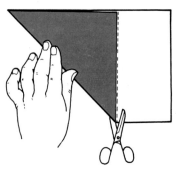

4 To complete, open out the triangle into . . .

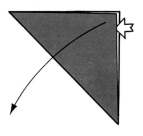

5 a square.

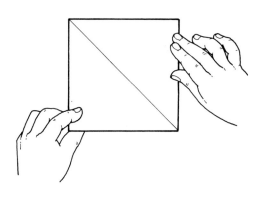

Christmas star

Stationery/tree decoration

Here is a very simple way to make a star. It will look most beautiful when made out of shining metallic foil (the kind that is used for gift wrapping).

You will need:

3 squares of paper the same size, coloured on one side and white on the other
Glue
Needle and cotton

1 Turn one square round so that it looks like a diamond, with the white side on top. Fold it in half from . . .

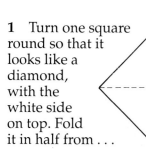

2 bottom to top, so making . . .

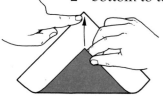

3 a triangle. Press the paper flat along its bottom edge, so making a shape that in origami is called the diaper fold.

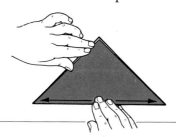

4 Repeat steps 1 to 3 with the remaining two squares. Tuck one diaper fold . . .

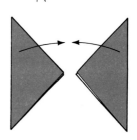

5 between the layers of another.

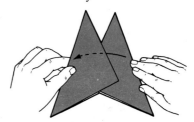

6 Turn the remaining diaper fold around so that it points towards you and place it on top of the other two as shown.

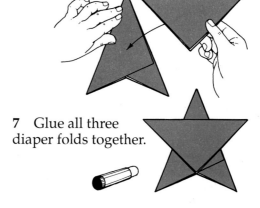

7 Glue all three diaper folds together.

8 To complete, attach a loop of cotton to the top of the star, so that you can hang it from the Christmas tree.

9

Paper hat 1

Party accessory

To make an origami hat that you can wear, use a square of paper that is the same size as one made from a broadsheet (large-sized) newspaper.

> **You will need:**
> Square of paper, coloured on one side and white on the other

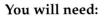

1 Begin by repeating steps 1 to 3 of the Christmas star on page 9.

2 Fold the right-hand side over to a point one-third of the way across the diaper fold.

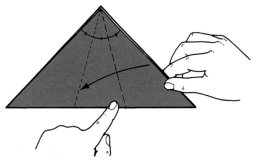

3 Fold the left-hand side over so that it lies on top.

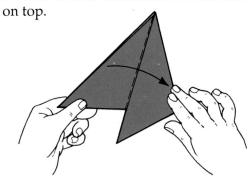

4 Fold the bottom points up as shown.

5 To complete, open the paper out . . .

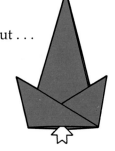

6 along the bottom edge.

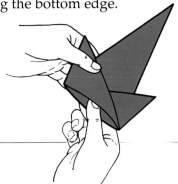

Paper hat 2

Party accessory

Here is another way to make a hat. If made from a sheet of colourful wrapping paper it will become a great hat to wear at a party.

You will need:
Square of paper, coloured on one side and white on the other

1 Begin by repeating steps 1 to 3 of the Christmas star on page 9. Turn the diaper fold round so that it points towards you.

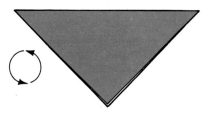

2 Fold and unfold the diaper fold in half from right to left.

3 Fold the right-hand half of the top edge over to a point one-third of the way across the diaper fold.

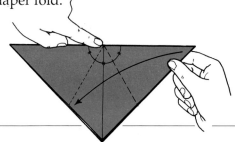

4 Fold the left-hand half of the top edge over so that it lies on top.

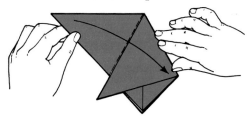

5 Fold the bottom points up as shown.

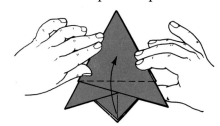

6 Fold the top layer of paper down and . . .

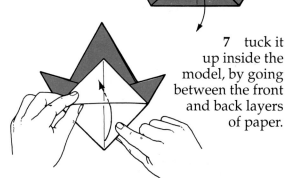

7 tuck it up inside the model, by going between the front and back layers of paper.

8 To complete, open out the paper along the bottom edge.

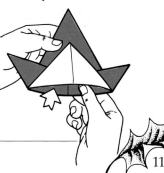

Christmas tree

Stationery/room decoration

Many models look most effective when they are displayed together. So why not try to make a display of Christmas trees?

You will need:
2 squares of paper the same size, coloured on one side and white on the other (try using a green one for the foliage and a brown one for the trunk)
Glue

1 *Foliage:* Turn the green square round so that it looks like a diamond, with the white side on top. Fold and unfold it in half from right to left.

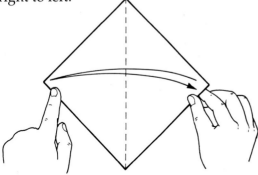

2 From the top point, fold the right-hand sloping side in to meet the middle fold-line.

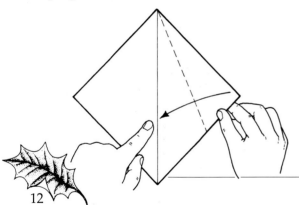

3 Press the paper flat.

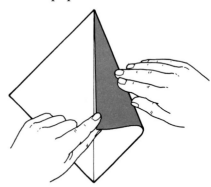

4 Repeat steps 2 and 3 with the left-hand sloping side, so making a shape that in origami is called the kite base.

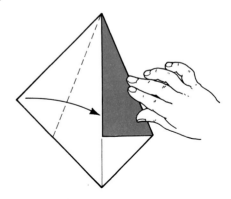

5 Fold the white triangle up along the base of the coloured triangle. Press the paper flat, so completing . . .

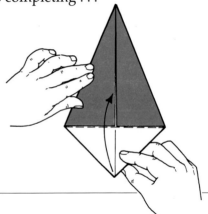

6 the foliage.

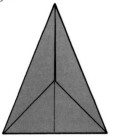

7 *Trunk:* Fold and unfold the brown square in half from right to left, with the white side on top.

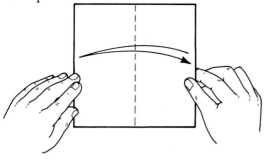

8 Fold the right-hand side in to meet the middle fold-line.

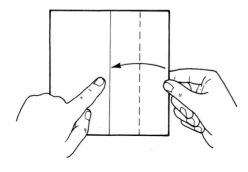

9 Repeat step 8 with the left-hand side, so making a shape that in origami is called the cupboard fold.

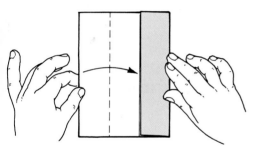

10 Fold the cupboard fold in half from right to left.

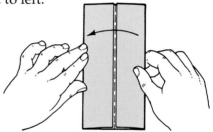

11 Press the paper flat, so completing the trunk.

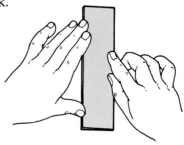

12 Glue the trunk on top of the foliage, into the position shown by the dotted lines.

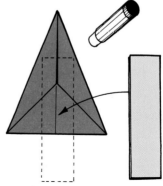

13 To complete, turn the model over. If you open out the base of the trunk a little, the Christmas tree will stand up by itself.

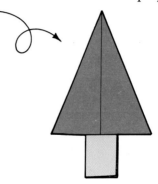

Candle

Stationery/wrapping decoration

This delightful model will make an ideal gift tag.

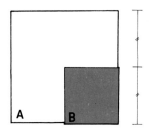

You will need:

2 squares of paper the same size, coloured on one side and white on the other (try using a white one for the candle and a yellow one for the flame)
Scissors
Glue

1 *Flame:* From the yellow square cut out square B to the size shown.

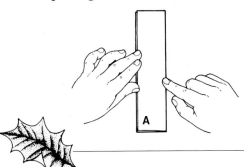

2 *Candle:* Begin by repeating steps 7 to 10 of the Christmas tree on page 13, with the white square. Press the paper flat, so completing the candle.

3 *Flame:* Begin by repeating steps 7 to 9 of the Christmas tree on page 13, with the yellow square. Fold the two bottom corners in to meet the middle edges.

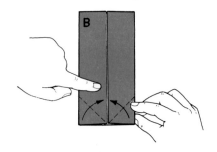

4 Fold the top over to lie along . . .

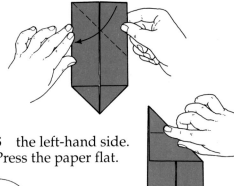

5 the left-hand side. Press the paper flat.

6 Turn the paper over, so completing the flame.

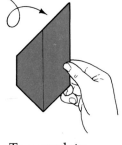

7 To complete, glue the flame into the top of the candle.

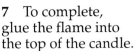

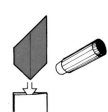

Holly decoration

Stationery/room/wrapping decoration

When made in miniature this model is ideal for gluing on to the front of an envelope.

You will need:

3 squares of paper all the same size, coloured on one side and white on the other (try using a red one for the berry and two dark green ones for the leaves)
Scissors
Glue

1 *Berry:* From the red square cut out square B to the size shown.

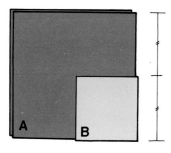

2 *Leaves:* Turn one dark green square round so that it looks like a diamond, with the white side on top. Fold and unfold it in half from right to left.

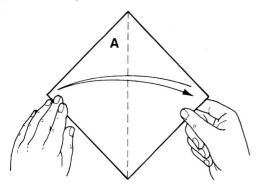

3 Fold and unfold the diamond in half from bottom to top.

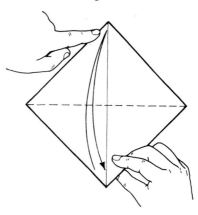

4 Fold the bottom point in to meet the middle.

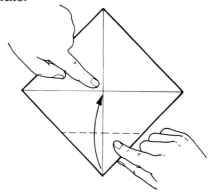

5 Repeat step 4 with the top point.

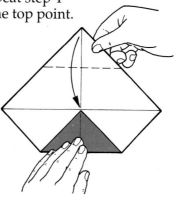

6 This should be the result. Press the paper flat, so making a leaf unit.

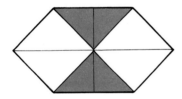

7 Turn the unit over. Repeat steps 2 to 7 with the remaining dark green square.

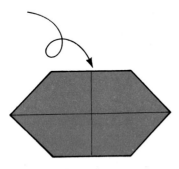

8 *Berry:* Begin by repeating steps 2 and 3, with the red square. Fold the right-hand corner to a point one-third of the way to the middle.

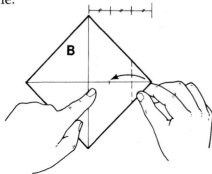

9 Fold the left-hand corner and the top and bottom points over to points one-third of the way to the middle.

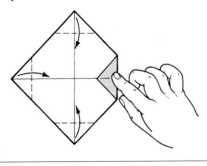

10 This should be the result. Press the paper flat.

11 Turn the paper over, so completing the berry.

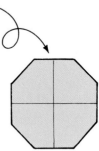

12 To complete, glue the berry on top of the leaves as shown.

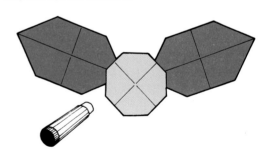

Mistletoe

Stationery/room/wrapping decoration

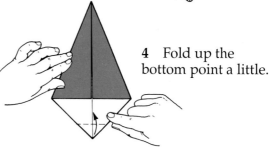

There is something special about plants that remain lush and green through the cold dark winter. So why not decorate your home with a few sprigs of origami mistletoe?

You will need:

3 squares of paper all the same size, coloured on one side and white on the other (try using a white one for the berry and two light green ones for the leaves)
Scissors
Glue

1 *Berry:* From the white square cut out square B to the size shown. Now, repeat steps 8 to 11 of the holly decoration on page 16.

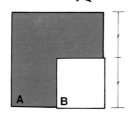

2 *Leaves:* Turn one light green square round so that it looks like a diamond, with the white side on top. Fold and unfold it in half from right to left.

3 From the top point, fold the sloping sides in to meet the middle fold-line, so making the kite base.

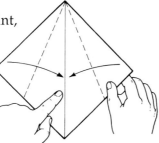

4 Fold up the bottom point a little.

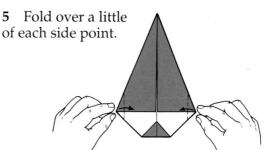

5 Fold over a little of each side point.

6 This should be the result. Press the paper flat, so making a leaf. Repeat steps 2 to 6 with the remaining light green square.

7 Turn the leaves over. To complete, glue the berry on top of the leaves, into the position shown by the dotted lines.

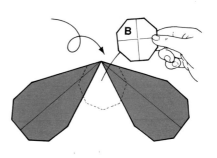

Three-dimensional candle

Table/tree decoration

Many models make ideal Christmas tree decorations. But to look really beautiful your model has to be neatly folded.

You will need:

2 squares of paper the same size, coloured on one side and white on the other (try using a white or stripy patterned one for the candle and a yellow one for the flame)
Scissors
Glue

1 *Flame:* From the yellow square cut out square B to the size shown.

2 *Candle:* Start to roll the white square into a tube from bottom to top (with the white side on top if you are using a stripy patterned one).

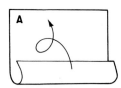

3 Continue to roll the paper into a tube. Near the end, glue the loose edge of paper to the tube, to prevent it from unravelling, so completing the candle.

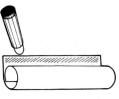

4 *Flame:* Turn the yellow square round so that it looks like a diamond, with the white side on top. Fold and unfold it in half from right to left.

5 From the top point, fold the sloping sides in to meet the middle fold-line, so making the kite base.

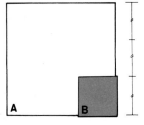

6 From the bottom point, fold the short sloping sides in to meet the middle fold-line, so making a shape that in origami is called the diamond base.

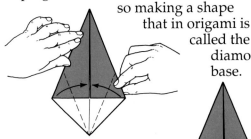

7 This should be the result. Press the paper flat, so completing the flame.

8 To complete, turn the flame over and glue it into the top of the candle. This model makes a perfect table decoration when it is glued inside a star-shaped box (see page 74).

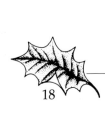

Christmas stocking

Stationery/room/tree decoration

One of the most delightful traditions of the season is hanging up a stocking in anticipation of Father Christmas's arrival on Christmas Eve. So here is a quick and easy way to make one.

> **You will need:**
> Square of paper, coloured on one side and white on the other
> Stapler
> Cotton

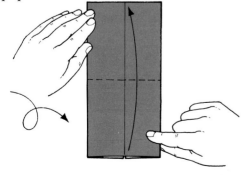

1 Begin by repeating steps 7 to 9 of the Christmas tree on page 13.

2 Turn the cupboard door fold over. Fold it in half from bottom to top, so making a flap of paper.

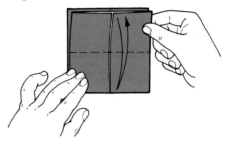

3 Fold and unfold the front flap in half from top to bottom.

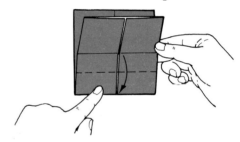

4 Pleat the front flap by folding it down, so that the fold-line made in step 3 . . .

5 lies along the bottom. Press the paper flat.

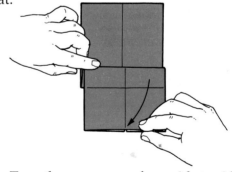

6 Turn the paper over from side to side. Fold it in half from left to right.

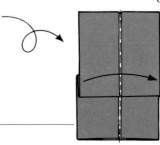

19

7 Hold the paper as shown and pull the bottom section of paper up . . .

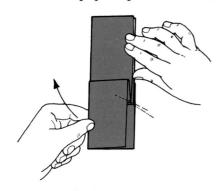

8 as far as the hidden pleat will allow you.

9 Fold over a little of the bottom section's top and bottom corners. Press the corners flat and unfold them.

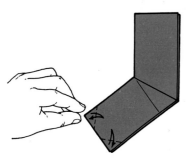

10 Inside reverse fold the top corner. This is what you do: place your thumb into the corner's groove and with your forefinger on top, pull the corner down inside the model, along the fold-lines made in step 9.

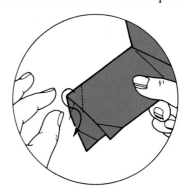

11 Fold the bottom corners up inside the model, along the fold-lines made in step 9. Press the model flat.

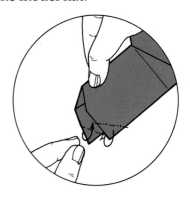

12 To complete, attach a loop of cotton to the top of the Christmas stocking, so that you can hang it from the Christmas tree.

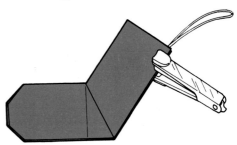

Father Christmas's boot

Stationery/wrapping decoration

This model makes a perfect gift tag or decoration.

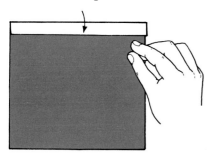

You will need:
Square of paper, coloured on one side and white on the other

1 Fold down a little of the top, with the coloured side on top.

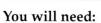

2 Repeat steps 7 to 9 of the Christmas tree on page 13.

3 Repeat steps 2 to 5 of the Christmas stocking on page 19.

4 Turn the paper over. Fold each bottom corner in to meet the pleat.

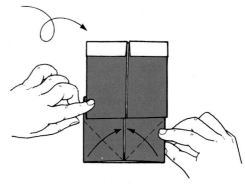

5 Fold the paper in half from left to right.

6 Repeat steps 7 to 8 of the Christmas stocking on page 20.

7 To complete, press the paper flat.

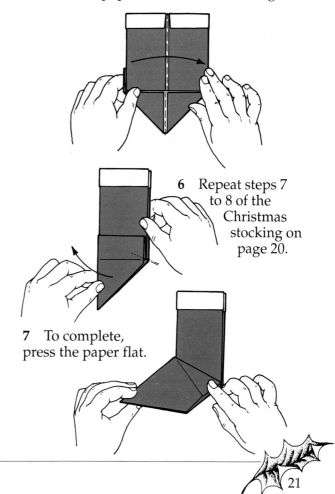

Christmas pudding

Stationery/wrapping decoration

Why not make some delicious looking puddings to give to your friends as Christmas cards? This model is a bit fiddly to make, but is well worth the effort.

You will need:

4 squares of paper all the same size, coloured on one side and white on the other (try using a red one and a dark green one for the holly decoration, a white one for the cream and a brown one for the pudding)
Pencil
Scissors
Glue

1 *Holly decoration:* From the red square cut out square A and from the dark green one two squares B, to the sizes shown.

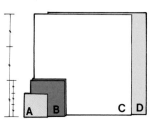

2 Repeat steps 2 to 12 of the holly decoration on pages 15-16 with the red and dark green squares.

3 *Cream:* Using the pencil, mark out this cream design on to the square of white paper as shown. Carefully cut around your pencil line. Put the lower part to one side as it is not required.

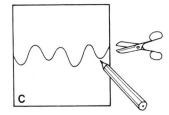

4 *Pudding:* Glue the cream on to the brown square as shown, with the coloured side on top.

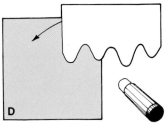

5 Turn the paper over. Fold the opposite corners and points together in turn to mark the diagonal fold-lines, then open up again.

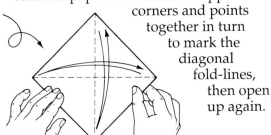

6 Fold the corners and the points over to points one-third of the way to the middle.

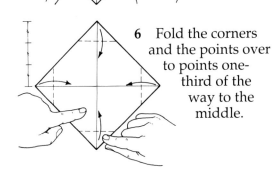

7 Turn the paper over. To complete, glue the holly decoration on to the Christmas pudding at an attractive angle.

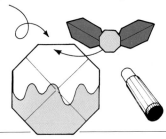

House with a chimney

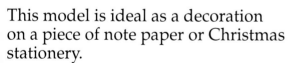

Stationery decoration

This model is ideal as a decoration on a piece of note paper or Christmas stationery.

> **You will need:**
> Square of paper, coloured on one side and white on the other

1 Fold the square in half from top to bottom, with the white side on top, so making a shape that in origami is called the book fold.

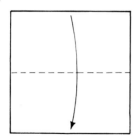

2 Fold and unfold the book fold in half from right to left.

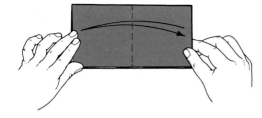

3 Fold the right and left-hand sides in to meet the middle fold-line.

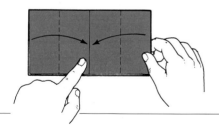

4 Lift the right-hand side up.

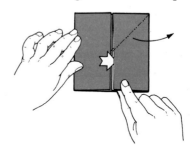

5 Insert your fingers between the layers of paper. Open them out and with your free hand, press down the top into the shape of a triangular roof. Press the paper flat.

6 Repeat steps 4 . . .

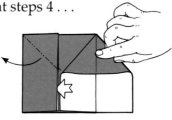

7 and 5 with the left-hand side, so making the traditional origami house.

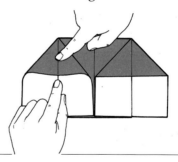

8 Turn the house over. Fold it in half from left to right.

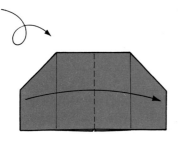

9 Fold the top left-hand point in to meet the middle and then . . .

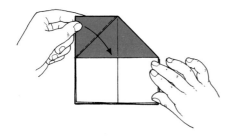

10 fold it up, so making . . .

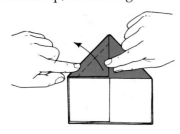

11 a small pleat. Press the paper flat.

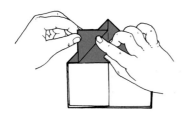

12 Tuck the pleat inside the model, by going between the front and . . .

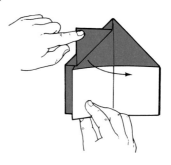

13 back left-hand layers of paper. Press the paper flat.

14 Here is the completed house with a chimney.

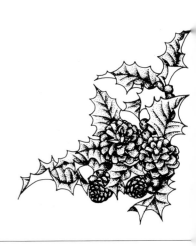

Church

Stationery/room decoration

This model is a perfect example of how, with just a few folds, you can make a complex looking piece of origami.

You will need:
Square of paper, coloured on one side and white on the other
Scissors
Glue

1 Cut the square in half from side to side, so making two rectangles. From one rectangle cut out square A to the size shown. Put the excess material to one side as it is not required.

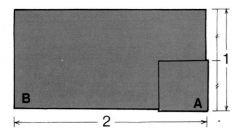

2 *Spire:* Begin by repeating steps 4 to 6 of the three-dimensional candle on page 18 with square A. Press the paper flat, so completing the spire.

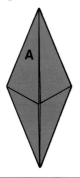

3 *Church:* Place the remaining rectangle sideways on, with the white side on top. Fold it in half from left to right, so making a flap of paper.

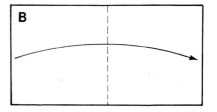

4 Fold the front flap over to a point one-third of the way to the left.

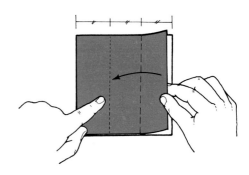

5 Fold the front flap in half from right to left.

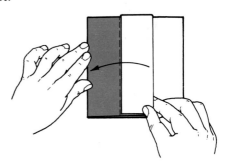

6 Fold the top layers of paper over to the left, as though turning a page of a book.

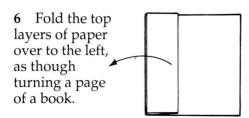

7 Fold the top over to lie along the left-hand side. Being careful to . . .

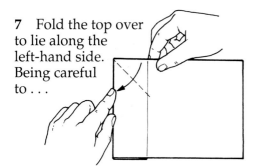

8 press the paper only as shown. Unfold the paper back to the beginning of step 7.

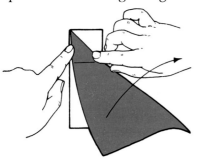

9 Fold the top over as far as shown, while at the same time . . .

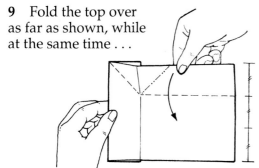

10 turning the page of the book back over . . .

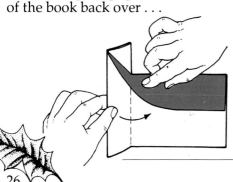

11 along the existing vertical fold-line. Press the paper flat.

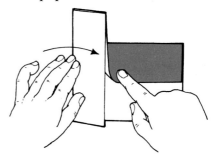

12 Turn the paper over. Fold over a little of the left-hand side.

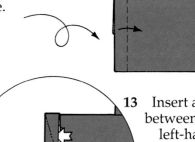

13 Insert a finger between the top left-hand layers of paper. Open them out and with your free hand . . .

14 press the paper down into the shape of a sloping triangular roof.

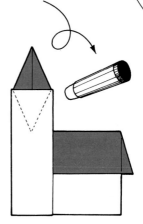

15 Turn the paper over. To complete, glue the spire into the top of the church's tower.

Father Christmas napkin ring

Stationery/tree/table decoration

Do try to fold this model accurately. Otherwise your finished napkin ring will not look neat and tidy.

You will need:

12cm square of paper, red on one side and white on the other
Glue
Small circle of white paper
Felt tip-pen
A 3cm x 15cm rectangle of card
Scissors
Napkin

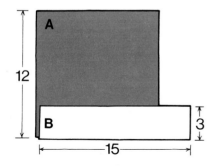

1 *Father Christmas:* Begin by repeating steps 1 to 4 of the Christmas tree on page 12, with the red square. Fold the kite base in half from bottom to top.

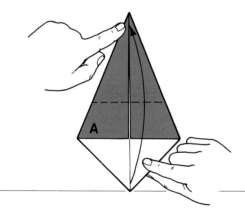

2 Fold the topmost layer of paper down to meet the bottom, so making a white triangle.

3 Fold the topmost layer of paper down on a line between the two side points.

4 Fold the white triangle's tip up and then down, so making . . .

5 a small pleat in the paper.

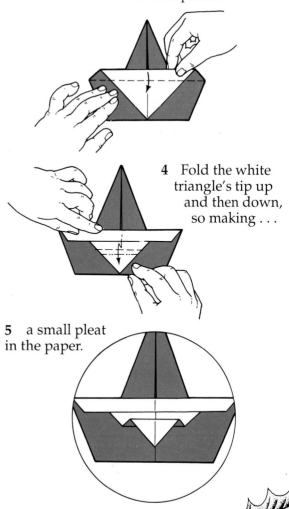

6 Turn the paper over. Fold the right and left-hand side points over the triangle as shown.

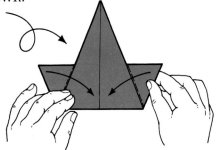

7 Glue the side points to the triangle, so preventing them from unfolding.

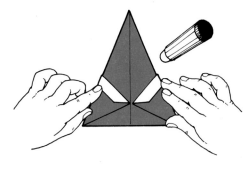

8 Turn the paper over. Fold the top point over, into the position shown by the dotted lines, so making a hat.

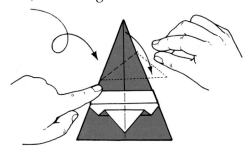

9 To suggest a pompom, glue the small circle of white paper on to the hat's point. Draw the eyes on with a felt-tip pen, so completing Father Christmas.

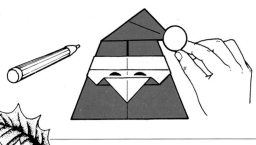

10 *Napkin ring:* Turn the rectangle round so that it is sideways on. On the upper left-hand side, cut a slit half way across the rectangle. Repeat on the lower right-hand side.

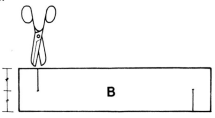

11 Bring the right-hand slit over to meet the left-hand slit and . . .

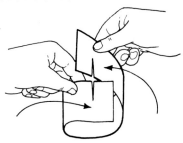

12 slip them one into the other, so that they are linked together. Glue Father Christmas on to the linked section.

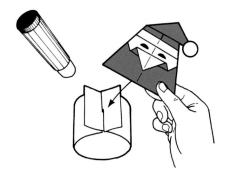

13 To complete, roll the napkin up and insert it into the napkin ring. Why not make another napkin ring and glue on a different origami model?

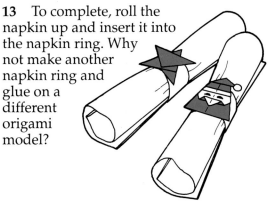

Bell

Stationery/wrapping decoration

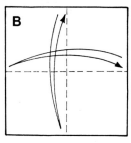

Made out of shiny metallic wrapping paper, this easy model makes an ideal decoration or gift tag.

You will need:

2 squares of paper the same size, coloured on one side and white on the other (try using a gold one for the bell and a silver one for the clapper)
Scissors
Glue

1 *Clapper:* From the silver square cut out square A to the size shown.

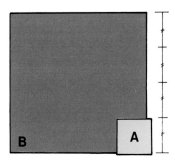

2 Turn the square round so that it looks like a diamond, with the white side on top. Fold the opposite corners and points together in turn to mark the diagonal fold-lines, then open up again. Fold the corners and the bottom point over to points one-third of the way to the middle. Turn the paper over, so completing the clapper.

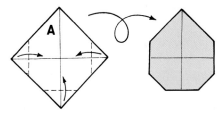

3 *Bell:* Fold and unfold the gold square in half from bottom to top and side to side, with the white side on top.

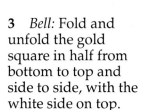

4 Fold the bottom in to meet . . .

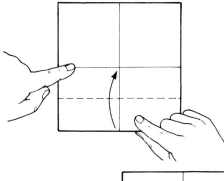

5 the middle. Press the paper flat.

6 Turn the paper over. Pleat the paper by folding the bottom in to meet the horizontal fold-line, while at the same time . . .

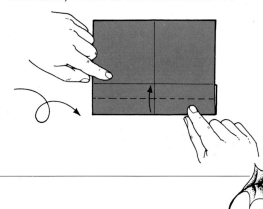

7 letting the paper from underneath flick up.

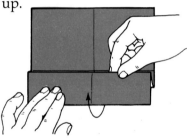

8 Turn the paper over. Fold the sides in to meet the middle.

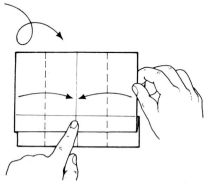

9 Pinch the topmost bottom right-hand layer of paper and . . .

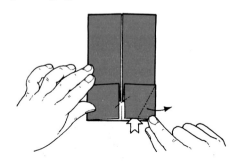

10 pull it across to the right as far as the hidden pleat will allow you.

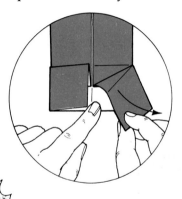

11 This should be the result. Repeat steps 9 to 10 with the topmost bottom left-hand layer of paper, pulling it across to the left in step 10. Press the paper flat.

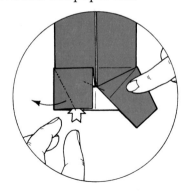

12 Fold over a little of each top corner.

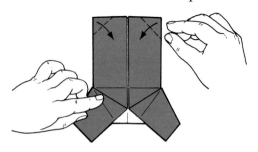

13 Turn the paper over. Tuck the two white triangles up inside the model, by going between the front and back layers of paper.

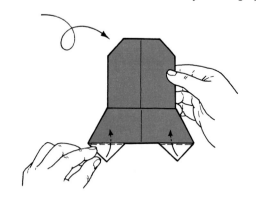

14 To complete, glue the clapper on to the bottom of the bell at an attractive angle.

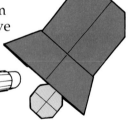

Place card stand

Table decoration/party accessory

This very simple, practical model is ideal as a place card, menu display stand or even as a memo stand.

You will need:
Square of paper, coloured on one side and white on the other
Small rectangle of card
Felt-tip pen

1   Begin by repeating steps 7 to 9 of the Christmas tree on page 13, but with the coloured side on top in step 7. Turn the cupboard fold round, so that it is sideways on. Fold the middle edges out as shown, so making . . .

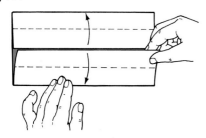

2   a pleat on either side of the paper.

3   Turn the paper over. Fold and unfold it in half from right to left.

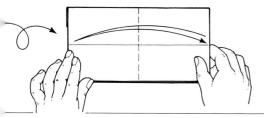

4   Fold the sides in to meet the middle, so making two flaps of paper.

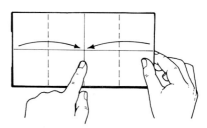

5   Tuck the inner top and bottom left-hand points behind their respective pleats.

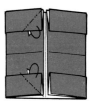

6   Tuck the right-hand flap underneath . . .

7   the pleats of the left-hand flap, so . . .

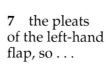

8   the paper becomes triangular and three-dimensional. Turn the model round into the position shown. To complete, write the name of your guest on the small rectangle of card and slip it behind the pleat's sloping edges.

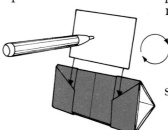

Fantasy napkin fold

Table decoration/party accessory

To decorate the Christmas table, try this simple napkin fold. If you use a cloth napkin, make sure that it is well starched, so that it can hold the folds.

You will need:
Paper or cloth napkin

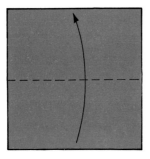

1 As a napkin is usually folded into quarters, open it out completely. Fold it in half from bottom to top.

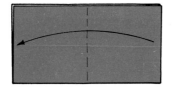

2 Fold the napkin in half from right to left, so making a flap.

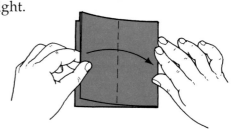

3 Fold the front flap in half from left to right.

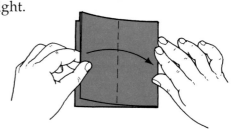

4 Once again fold the front flap in half from left to right. Press the flap flat. Open it out completely from left to right.

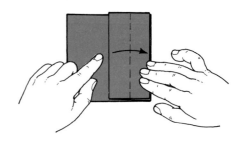

5 Along the existing right-hand fold-lines pleat the napkin backwards, forwards, backwards and forwards once more.

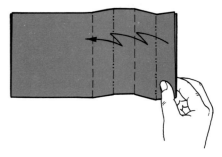

6 This should be the result. Press the napkin flat.

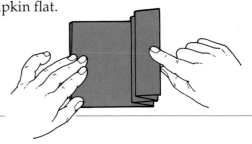

7   Turn the napkin over. Fold it in half from bottom to top.

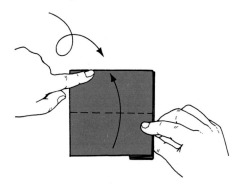

8   Fold the top down, laying it along the pleats.

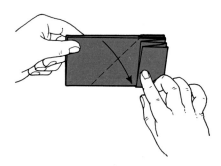

9   Fold the overlap at the bottom towards the back.

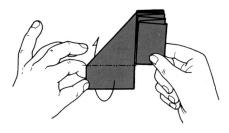

10   Rest the overlap on the table. Open out the pleats and arrange . . .

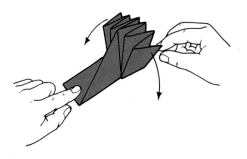

11   them into a fan. To complete, turn the napkin round into the position shown.

Cable napkin fold

Table decoration/party accessory

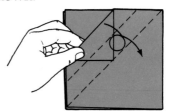

This second napkin fold has a pocket for silverware. It can be made with either a single napkin or two same-size, different coloured ones folded together.

> **You will need:**
> Paper or cloth napkin

1 As a napkin is usually folded into quarters ensure that the four loose corners are at upper left. Fold and unfold the napkin in half from top left to bottom right.

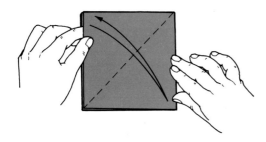

2 Fold the first top left-hand corner in to meet the middle fold-line.

3 Fold the newly-made edge over and over as shown.

4 Fold the second top left-hand corner down to meet the bottom right-hand corner and then . . .

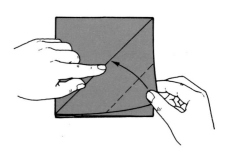

5 fold it in to meet the middle fold-line.

6 Repeat step 3.

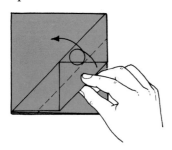

7 This should be the result. Press the napkin flat.

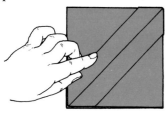

8 Turn the napkin over from top to bottom. Fold the bottom over to a point one-third of the way to the top.

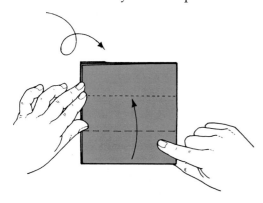

9 Fold the top down and tuck the top right-hand corner underneath the lower right-hand sloping edge as shown.

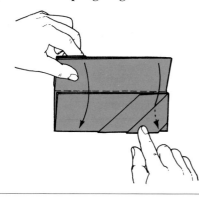

10 This should be the result. Press the napkin flat.

11 To complete, turn the napkin over.

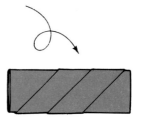

Crown

Party accessory

A while ago, when we were on holiday in Germany, the grandmother of the family we were staying with showed us how to fold this Christmas hat.

You will need:

Square of paper, coloured on one side and white on the other

1 Begin by repeating steps 1 to 7 of the house with a chimney on page 23.

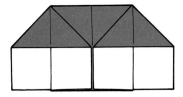

2 Turn the traditional house over. Fold the sides in to meet the middle fold-line.

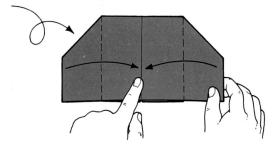

3 Fold the front flap of paper up to meet the top and then . . .

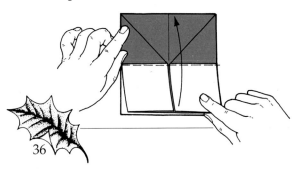

4 down in to the middle.

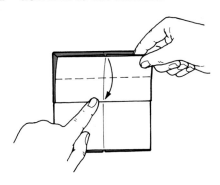

5 Insert a finger between the top right-hand layers of paper as shown. Open them out and . . .

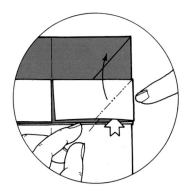

6 with your free hand, press the paper down into . . .

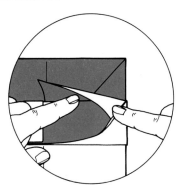

7   the shape of a triangular sloping roof.

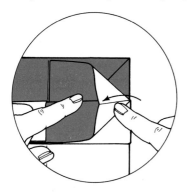

8   Fold the corner nearest to the sloping roof behind as shown.

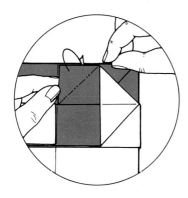

9   Repeat steps 5 to 8 with the top left-hand layer of paper.

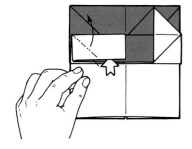

10   This should be the result. Press the paper flat.

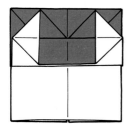

11   Turn the paper over. Repeat steps 3 to 10.

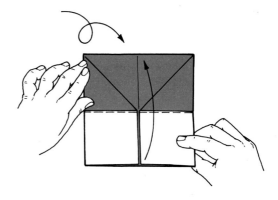

12   Open the paper out along the bottom edge.

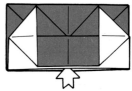

13   To complete, push the top in and shape the points of the crown.

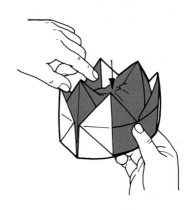

Cracker

Stationery decoration

Folding your own crackers is not difficult, and does mean that you can make an attractive item to decorate your Christmas stationery.

You will need:

Rectangle of paper, 2 x 1 in proportion, coloured on one side and white on the other

1   Place the rectangle sideways on, with the white side on top. Fold and unfold it in half from right to left.

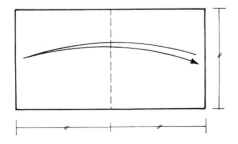

2   Fold and unfold the rectangle in half from bottom to top.

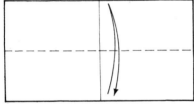

3   Fold the top and bottom in to meet the middle.

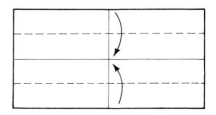

4   Turn the paper over. Fold the right-hand side in to meet the middle, so making a flap of paper.

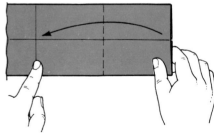

5   Fold and unfold the flap in half from side to side.

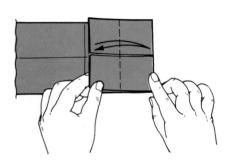

6 Fold the flap over, so that the fold-line made in step 5 . . .

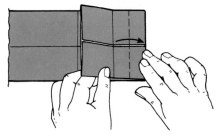

7 lies along the side nearest to it, so making a pleat.

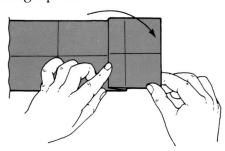

8 Turn the paper over. The pleat's inside layers have to be flattened down. This is what you do . . .

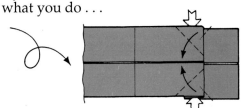

9 fold the pleat's 'lower' corner in towards the middle as shown, making . . .

10 the inside layer rise up.

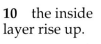

11 Flatten the folded edge of the layer to form a triangle as shown.

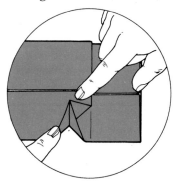

12 Repeat steps 9 to 11 with the pleat's 'upper' corner.

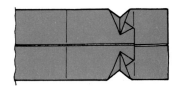

13 Turn the paper over. Fold the left-hand side in to meet the middle. Repeat steps 5 to 12.

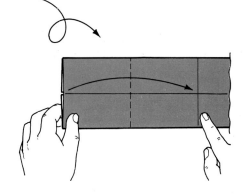

14 To complete, turn the model over.

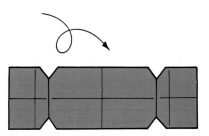

Snowman

Stationery/room decoration

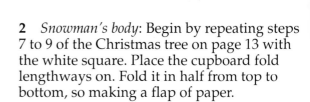

Even though this model may at first appear rather tricky, it is very easy. Remember, as with any fold, do look carefully at each illustration to see what you should do.

> **You will need:**
>
> 3 squares of paper all the same size, coloured on one side and white on the other (try using a white one for the snowman's body, a stripy patterned one for the scarf and a black one for the hat)
> Scissors
> Black felt-tip pen
> Small piece of orange paper
> Glue

1 From the stripy paper cut out square B and from the black paper cut out square C, to the sizes shown.

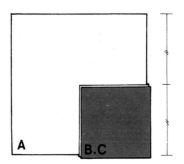

2 *Snowman's body*: Begin by repeating steps 7 to 9 of the Christmas tree on page 13 with the white square. Place the cupboard fold lengthways on. Fold it in half from top to bottom, so making a flap of paper.

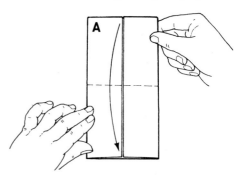

3 Fold and unfold the front flap in half from bottom to top.

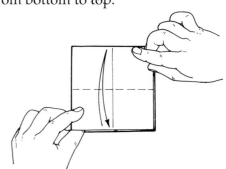

4 Fold the front flap up, so that the fold-line made in step 3 lies along the top, so making a pleat.

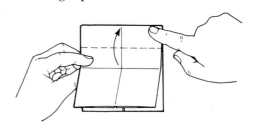

Above: **Christmas cards showing Church p25; Three-dimensional Christmas tree p103; Window card p101; Snowma**n p40; **Pop-up reindeer p103; for how to make Christmas cards** *see* p100

Below: **Christmas cards showing Poinsettia and heart p51; Pigeon p58; Father Christmas from Father Christmas nap**k**in**
ring p27; Bells p29; Holly decoration p15; Candle p14; Christmas stocking p19; Ribbon decoration p48; Mistletoe p1

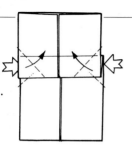

5 The pleat's inside layers have to be flattened down. This is what you do . . .

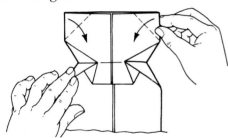

6 fold the pleat's 'lower' right-hand corner in towards the middle as shown, so making the inside layer rise up.

7 Flatten the folded edge of the layer to form a triangle. Repeat steps 6 and 7 with the pleat's 'lower' left-hand corner. Fold the top corners down as shown, so making two small triangles.

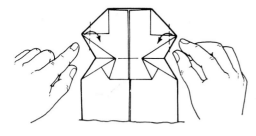

8 Fold a little of each side point inwards.

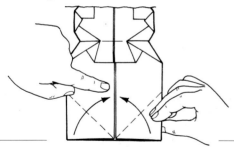

9 Fold each bottom corner in to meet the middle edges.

10 Fold the bottom point up as shown.

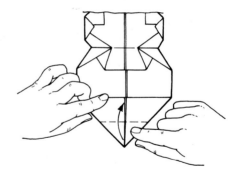

11 This should be the result. Press the paper flat.

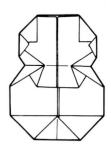

12 Turn the paper over, so completing the snowman's body.

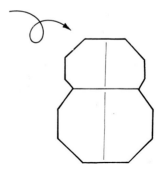

13 *Scarf:* Begin by repeating steps 7 to 9 of the Christmas tree on page 13, with the stripy square. Fold the cupboard fold in half from right to left, so completing the scarf.

B

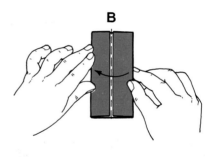

14 Draw on the snowman's eyes and buttons with a felt-tip pen. From the small piece of orange paper cut out a small carrot-like shape, to make the snowman's nose. Glue the nose on to the body as shown. Finally, glue one end of the scarf behind the horizontal pleat at an attractive angle.

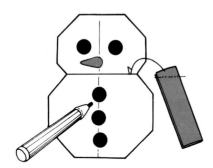

15 *Hat:* Begin by repeating steps 1 to 7 of the house with a chimney on page 23, with the black square, but with the coloured side on top in step 1.

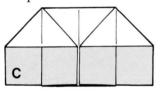

16 Turn the traditional house over from top to bottom. Fold and unfold the front flap of paper in half from top to bottom.

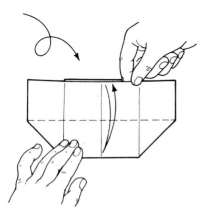

17 Fold the front flap down to meet the fold-line made in step 16, so making the hat's brim.

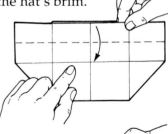

18 Fold the bottom up to meet the brim.

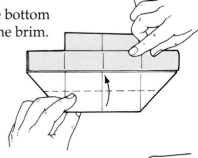

19 Fold the brim down along the fold-line made in step 16.

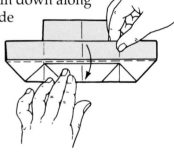

20 Here is the completed hat.

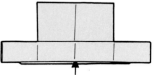

21 To complete, insert the snowman's head underneath the hat's brim, as shown by the arrow in step 20, and glue them together at an attractive angle.

Christmas chain

Room/tree decoration

This beautiful model is made by folding the same unit several times. The units are then fitted together. This style of folding is called modular origami.

You will need:

Several squares of paper all the same size, coloured on one side and white on the other
Glue

1 Begin by repeating steps 2 to 6 of the holly decoration on pages 15-16 with one square. Fold the top and bottom in to meet the middle.

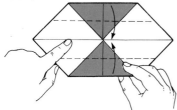

2 Turn the paper over. Fold the corners in to meet the middle, so making two flaps of paper.

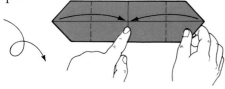

3 Fold the top behind to the bottom.

4 Pull the right-hand flap . . .

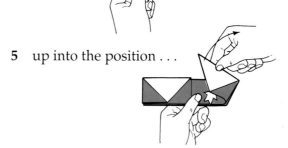

5 up into the position . . .

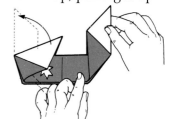

6 shown. Press the paper flat. Repeat steps 4 to 6 with the left-hand flap, pulling it up into the position shown by the dotted lines, so making one unit. Now fold a few more!

7 Assembly: Tuck one unit inside another and glue them together.

8 For a very colourful Christmas chain, carefully tuck, link and glue together lots of units. When hanging your chain, make sure that you tie or pin it up at frequent intervals, so that it will not fall apart.

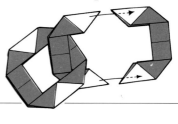

Snowflakes

Room decoration

The beauty of these models lies in the lines and shadows that are created by the folding. For a very stunning effect, when held up to the light, try making them out of squares of tissue paper.

You will need:

Several squares of paper all the same size, coloured on one side and white on the other
Glue

1 *Six point snowflake:* Begin by repeating steps 2 to 6 of the holly decoration on pages 15-16 with six squares.

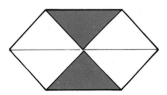

2 Arrange the units one on top of the other as shown. Glue them together, so completing the six point snowflake.

3 *Eight point snowflake:* Begin by repeating step 1 with eight squares. From the right-hand corner of each unit, fold the top and bottom sloping sides in to meet the middle fold-line.

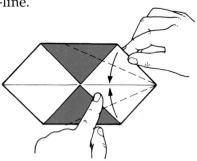

4 Arrange the units one on top of the other as shown. Glue them together . . .

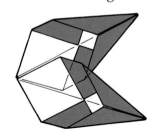

5 so completing the eight point snowflake.

6 *Sixteen point snowflake:* Begin by repeating step 3 with sixteen squares. Arrange the units one on top of the other as shown. Glue them together . . .

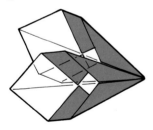

7 so completing the sixteen point snowflake.

8 *Variation:* Begin by repeating step 1 with eight squares. Fold over a little of the right-hand corner of each unit.

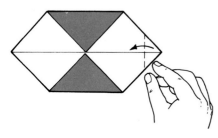

9 Fold what is remaining of the top and bottom right-hand sloping sides in to meet the middle fold-line.

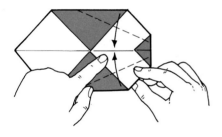

10 From the left-hand corner of each unit, fold the bottom sloping side in to meet the middle fold-line.

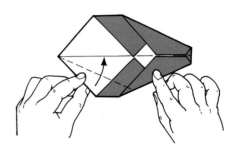

11 Arrange the units one on top of the other as shown. Glue them together . . .

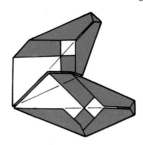

12 so completing the variation. Using the techniques already learned, see what new snowflakes you can create.

Reindeer

Stationery/room decoration

Once you have learned how to fold this model you can make it your own by changing around the angle of the head and tail.

You will need:

Square of paper, coloured on one side and white on the other
Piece of thin card
Small circle of brown card
Scissors
Glue

1 Turn the square round so that it looks like a diamond, with the white side on top. Fold and unfold it in half from bottom to top.

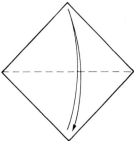

2 From the left-hand corner fold the top and bottom sloping sides in to meet the middle fold-line, so making the kite base.

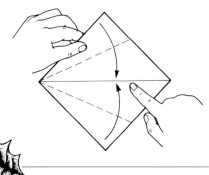

3 Fold the right-hand corner over to meet the base of the coloured triangle. Press the corner flat and unfold it.

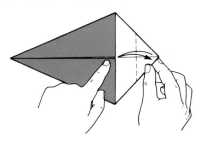

4 Turn the kite base over. Fold the left-hand point over to where the fold-lines meet.

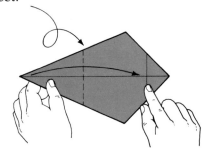

5 Fold the point back over to meet the left-hand side.

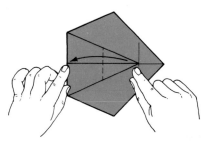

6 Fold behind a little of the point, so making the reindeer's head and neck.

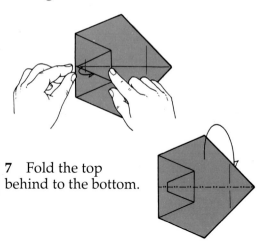

7 Fold the top behind to the bottom.

8 Pull the head and neck up and press them flat, into the position shown in step 9.

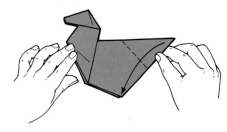

9 Fold the right-hand point down to meet the bottom point.

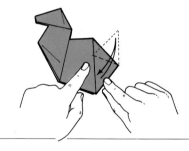

10 Fold the point back up, into the position shown by the dotted lines. Press the point flat and unfold it.

11 Now inside reverse fold the right-hand point. This is what you do . . .

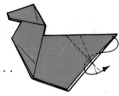

12 using the fold-lines made in step 9 as a guide, push the right-hand point down inside the model as shown.

13 Using the fold-lines made in step 10 as a guide, pull the point up as shown. Press the paper flat, so making the tail.

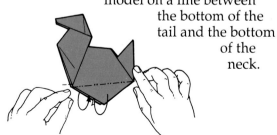

14 Fold the bottom points up inside the model on a line between the bottom of the tail and the bottom of the neck.

15 From the piece of thin card cut out a set of antlers. Glue them inside the head as shown. To complete, glue the small circle of brown card on to the front of the head, so suggesting the reindeer's nose. Remember, if you want to make Rudolf use a circle of red card for his glowing nose.

Ribbon decoration

Stationery/room decoration

When making this model try hard to find a beautiful square of paper as this will enhance the finished item.

You will need:
Square of paper, coloured on one side and white on the other
Scissors
Glue

1 Fold and unfold the square in half from bottom to top, with the coloured side on top. Cut along the middle fold-line, so making rectangles A and B.

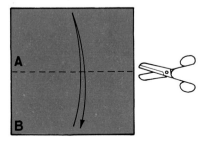

2 *Tails:* Place rectangle A sideways on, with the coloured side on top. Fold it in half from bottom to top, so making a flap of paper.

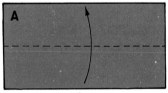

3 Fold the front flap in half from top to bottom.

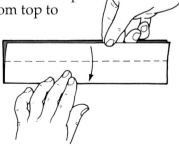

4 This should be the result. Press the paper flat.

5 Turn the paper over. Fold and unfold it in half from top to bottom.

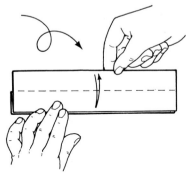

6 From the top corner, fold the bottom right-hand corner up to meet the middle fold-line, so making . . .

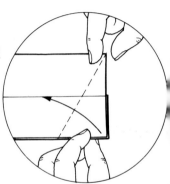

7 a triangle. Insert a finger underneath the triangle's top layer. Open it out and . . .

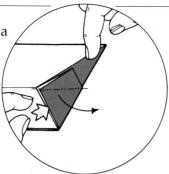

8 with your free hand, press it down neatly as shown.

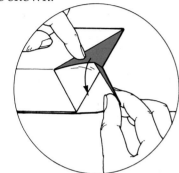

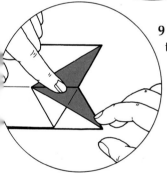

9 This should be the result. Repeat steps 6 to 8 with the bottom left-hand corner.

10 Fold the right side behind to the left side, so making a flap.

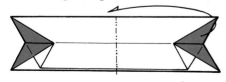

11 Repeat step 6.

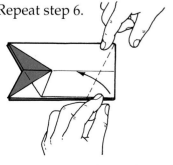

12 Fold the front flap over to the right. But do *not* unfold step 11.

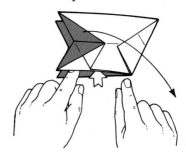

13 Turn the paper round, into the position as shown. Fold the top point behind. Press the paper flat, so completing the tails.

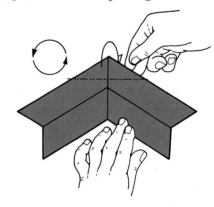

14 *Bow:* Place rectangle B sideways on, with the white side on top. Fold it in half from right to left.

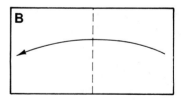

15 Fold the right-hand side over to a point one-third of the way to the left.

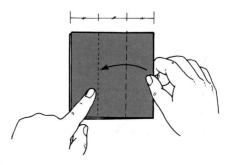

16 Fold the 'middle' folded edge over to meet the right-hand side. Press the paper flat. Open it out completely.

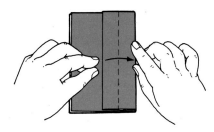

17 Along the fold-lines made in steps 15 and 16, pleat the paper on either side of the middle fold-line, with the white side on top.

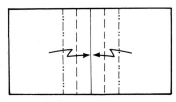

18 Fold the bottom up to a point one third of the way to the top.

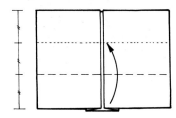

19 Fold the right-hand layer of paper down as shown.

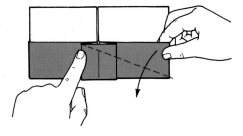

20 Repeat step 19 with the left-hand layer of paper.

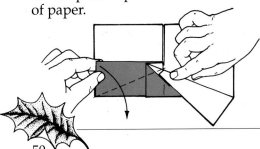

21 Fold the top down to meet the visible horizontal edge. Repeat steps 19 and 20, folding up instead of down.

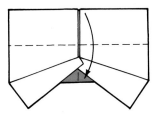

22 This should be the result. Press the paper flat.

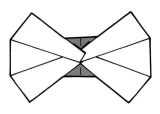

23 Turn the paper over. To complete, glue the bow on to the tails at an attractive angle.

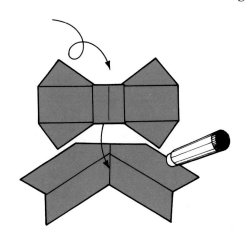

Poinsettia and heart

Stationery/room decoration

The poinsettia is the Christmas flower in North America. Native to Mexico, it is called the flower of the Holy Night there.

You will need:

10 squares of paper all the same size, coloured on one side and white on the other (try using eight green ones for the poinsettia's leaves, two red ones for its centre)
Scissors
Glue

1 *Centre:* Begin by repeating step 1 of the ribbon decoration on page 48 with the two red squares, so making four rectangles.

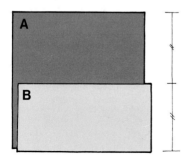

2 *Leaves:* Begin by repeating steps 7 to 9 of the Christmas tree on page 13 with the eight green squares.

3 Turn one cupboard fold over, placing it sideways on. Pleat the paper by folding the bottom in to meet the middle fold-line, while at the same time . . .

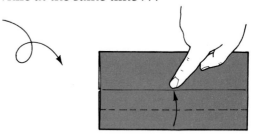

4 letting the paper from underneath flick up.

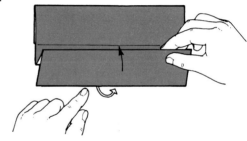

5 Repeat steps 3 and 4 with the top. But do *not* turn the paper over, as in the beginning of step 3.

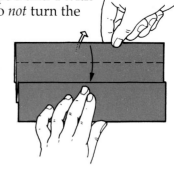

6 This should be the result. Press the paper flat.

7 Turn the paper over. Fold the top left-hand and the top and bottom right-hand corners in to meet the middle fold-line.

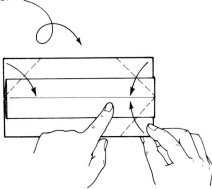

8 This should be the result. Press the paper flat.

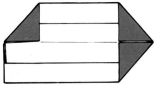

9 Turn the paper over. Fold the top left-hand corner in to meet the middle folded edges, so making a triangle.

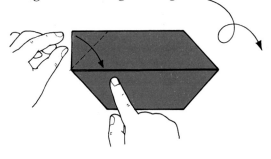

10 Fold the triangle's tip up to meet its base.

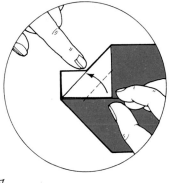

11 Return what is left of the corner back to its original position, so completing one leaf.

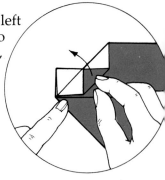

12 *Assembly:* Repeat steps 3 to 11 with the remaining seven squares. Tuck one leaf inside another as shown. Glue them together.

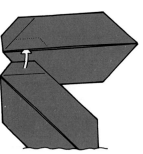

13 Keep on tucking and gluing leaves together carefully, until you have built up this leaf design.

14 *Centre:* Place one red rectangle sideways on, with the white side on top. Fold it in half from right to left.

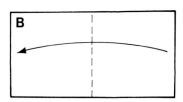

15 Fold and unfold the paper in half from top right to bottom left.

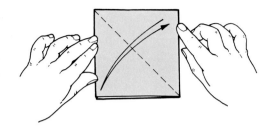

16 Fold the right-hand side in to lie along the fold-line made in step 15. Press the side flat and unfold it.

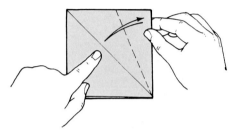

17 Fold the right-hand side in to lie along the fold-line made in step 16. Press the side flat and unfold it.

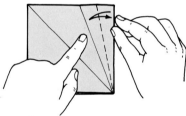

18 Open out the paper completely. Along the fold-lines made in steps 16 and 17, pleat the paper on either side of the middle fold-line, with the white side on top.

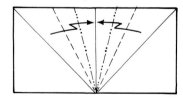

19 Fold the bottom right and left-hand sloping edges in to lie along the fold-lines made in step 15.

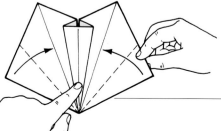

20 Fold over a little of each side point and the middle points.

21 Turn the paper over, so completing one centre unit. Repeat steps 14 to 21 with the remaining three red rectangles.

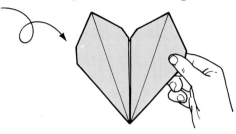

22 *Poinsettia assembly:* Arrange the centre units side by side on top of the leaves as shown. To complete, glue the centre units and leaves together.

23 *Heart:* Take another red square and repeat step 1. Put one rectangle to one side as it is not required. With the remaining one, repeat steps 14 to 20. Now, fold over a little of each top point.

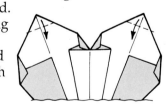

24 To complete, turn the model over.

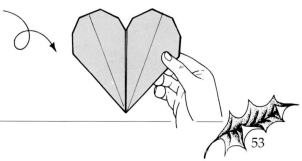

Windmill gift tag

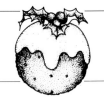

Room/table/tree/wrapping decoration

When carefully folded out of coloured paper, this model looks perfect glued on to a gift box, or it could be used as a drinks mat.

You will need:
Square of paper, coloured on one side and white on the other
Glue
2 thin strips of paper
Bow (see page 49)

1   Fold the opposite corners and points together in turn to mark the diagonal fold-lines, with the white side on top, then open up again.

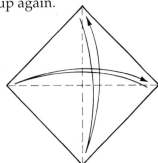

2   Fold the bottom point in to meet the middle, so making a coloured triangle.

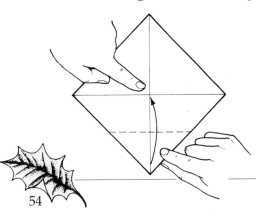

3   Fold and unfold the triangle in half from top to bottom.

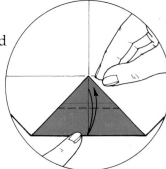

4   Fold the triangle's tip down to meet the fold-line made in step 3.

5   Fold the newly-made edge down along the fold-line made in step 3.

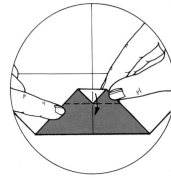

6   Fold the newly-made edge in to meet the middle.

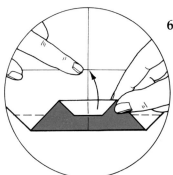

7 Fold the right-hand corner over as far as shown.

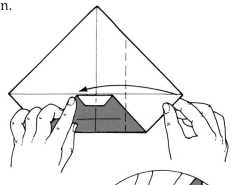

8 Fold the corner to where the horizontal fold-line and the underneath vertical fold-line meet.

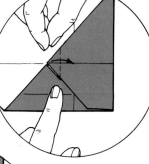

9 Fold the newly-made edge over on a line that runs along the underneath vertical fold-line.

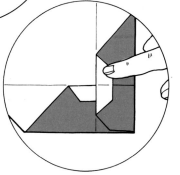

10 This should be the result. Press the paper flat. Repeat steps 7 to 10 with the top point and left-hand corner.

11 Fold down the front flap of paper.

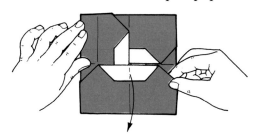

12 Refold the front flap over along the existing horizontal fold-line, while at the same time sliding its right-hand half underneath the bottom right-hand flap of paper as shown.

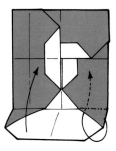

13 Here is the completed windmill gift tag.

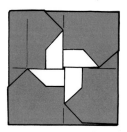

14 To convert the gift tag into a parcel tag, turn it over and glue the two thin strips along the middle fold-lines as shown. Fold the ends of the strips behind and glue them down. Should the ends protrude over the edges of the parcel, cut them off.

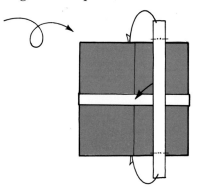

15 To complete, glue on the bow at an attractive angle.

Gift box

Wrapping/table decoration

This model is very easy to make. Do not be discouraged by the tricky folds in steps 6 to 11; they all fall into place very easily.

> **You will need:**
> 2 squares of paper the same size, coloured on one side and white on the other

1 *Base:* Fold and unfold one square in half from bottom to top and side to side, with the coloured side on top.

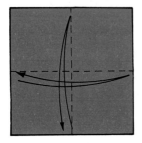

2 Turn the paper over and round so that it looks like a diamond. Fold the corners in to meet the middle, so making a shape that in origami is called the blintz base.

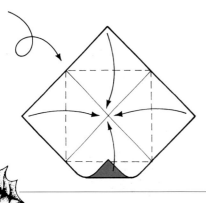

3 Fold the top and bottom in to meet the middle. Press them flat and unfold them.

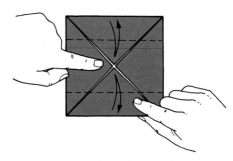

4 Repeat step 3 with the sides.

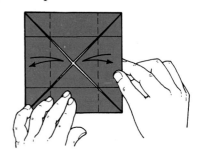

5 Unfold the two middle corners as shown.

6 Using the existing fold-lines . . .

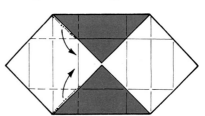

7 form the left-hand side of the base.

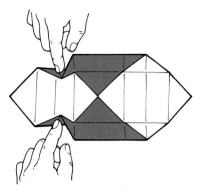

8 Turn the model round into the position shown. Once again using the existing fold-lines, fold the side . . .

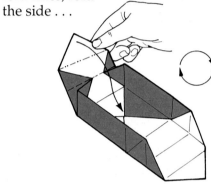

9 into the base, so locking all the folds together.

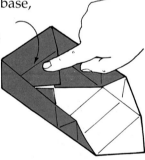

10 Repeat steps 6 and 7 at the opposite end of the paper, to form the right-hand side of the base.

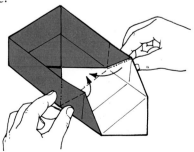

11 Repeat steps 8 and 9.

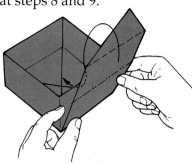

12 Here is the completed base.

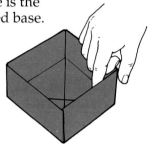

13 *Lid*: Repeat steps 1 to 11 with the remaining square, but in steps 3 and 4 fold the top and bottom and the sides slightly short of the middle, as shown.

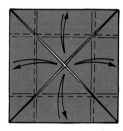

14 Here is the completed lid.

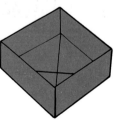

15 *Assembly:* Turn the lid over and slide it over the base, so completing the gift box.

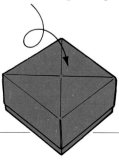

Pigeon

Stationery

Try changing the angle of the head, tail and wings each time you fold this model to see how many different pigeons you can create.

You will need:
Square of paper, coloured on one side and white on the other

1 Turn the square round so that it looks like a diamond, with the white side on top. Fold it in half from top to bottom, so making an upside-down diaper fold.

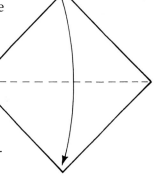

2 Fold the diaper fold in half from right to left.

3 Fold the front left-hand point down to meet the bottom point, so making a triangular flap.

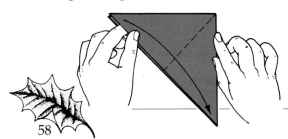

4 Repeat step 3 with the remaining left-hand point, folding it behind as shown.

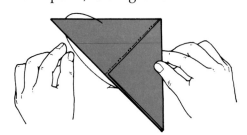

5 Fold the top point over to meet the left-hand side points. Press the point flat and unfold it.

6 Fold the front flap up along the fold-line made in step 5, so opening out the adjoining side point.

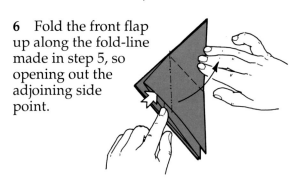

7 With you free hand press the side point down into the shape of a triangular roof as shown, so making a wing.

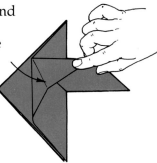

8 Turn the paper over from right to left. Repeat steps 6 and 7.

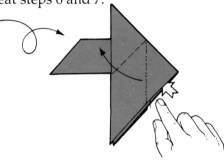

9 Open out the bottom triangular point and . . .

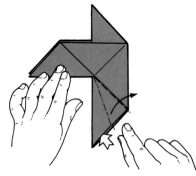

10 press it down into a diamond as shown, so making the tail.

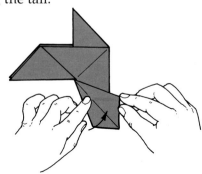

11 Turn the paper round into the position shown. Now inside reverse fold the right-hand triangular point. This is what you do . . .

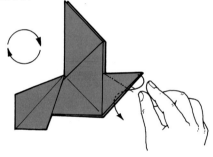

12 place your thumb into the point's groove, and . . .

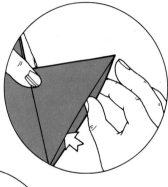

13 with your forefinger on top, pull the point down . . .

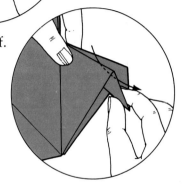

14 inside itself. Press the paper flat, so making the head and beak.

15 Fold the front wing down and then back up, so making a small pleat.

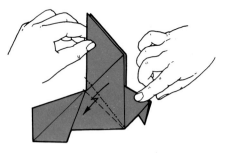

16 Here is the completed pigeon.

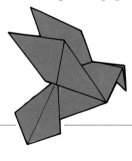

Robin

Stationery/room decoration

When making this model, try hard to find the right colour and texture of paper, as this will enhance the finished item and make it look more realistic.

You will need:

3 squares of paper all the same size, coloured on one side and white on the other (try using a yellow one for the beak and feet, an orange one for the body and a brown one for the wings)
Felt-tip pen
Glue

1   From the yellow square cut out squares A and B to the sizes shown.

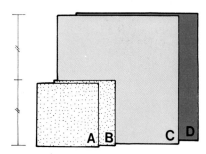

2   *Beak:* Turn one yellow square round so that it looks like a diamond, with the white side on top. Fold it in half from bottom to top, so making a diaper fold.

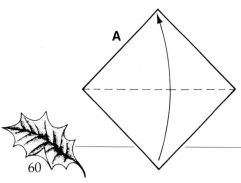

3   Fold the diaper fold in half from left to right.

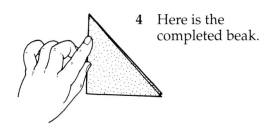

4   Here is the completed beak.

5   *Feet:* Begin by repeating step 2, with the remaining yellow square. Fold the right-hand point over, into the position shown by the dotted lines. Press the paper flat, so completing the feet.

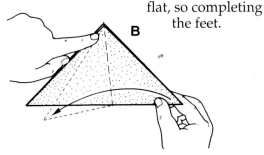

6   *Body:* Turn the orange square round so that it looks like a diamond, with the white side on top. Fold it in half from top to bottom, so completing the body.

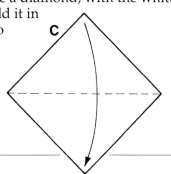

7 *Wings:* Begin by repeating steps 2 to 6 of the holly decoration on pages 15-16 with the brown square. Fold the unit in half from top to bottom, so completing the wings.

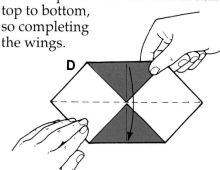

8 *Assembly:* Tuck the body inside the wings.

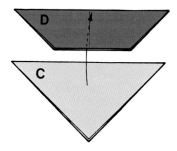

9 Turn the paper round into the position as shown. Fold a little of the body's bottom points up inside.

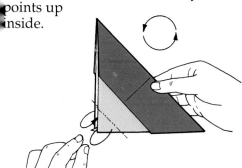

10 Fold the top point down to meet the top of the body. Press the point flat and unfold it.

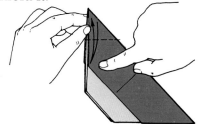

11 Push the top point down inside the model along the fold-lines made in step 10, so making an inside reverse fold.

12 Turn the beak round into the position as shown. Tuck the beak's triangular flaps round the reversed point.

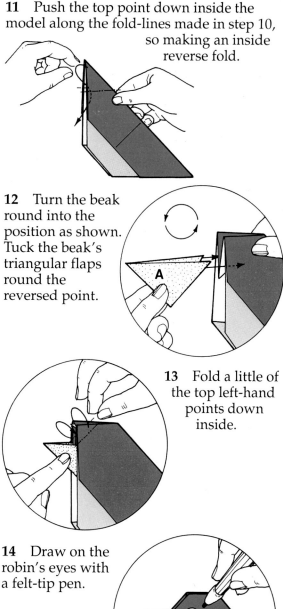

13 Fold a little of the top left-hand points down inside.

14 Draw on the robin's eyes with a felt-tip pen.

15 To complete, glue the feet into the bottom of the robin at an attractive angle.

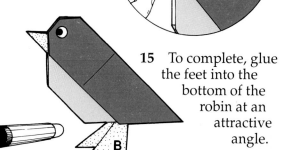

Three-dimensional star

Tree decoration

The following model is based around a very easy unit. Make it in a variety of colours for the best effect.

> **You will need:**
> 4 squares of paper all the same size, coloured on one side and white on the other
> Glue
> Needle and cotton

1 Begin by repeating steps 1 to 4 of the Christmas tree on page 12 with one square.

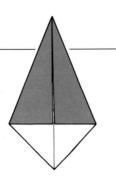

2 Turn the kite base round so that it points to the left. From the right-hand corner, fold the short sloping sides in to meet the middle fold-line. Press the sides flat and unfold them.

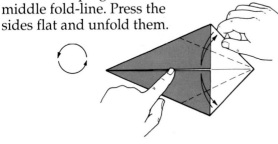

3 Fold the right-hand corner over on a line between the bottom point and where the upper sloping fold-line meets the top.

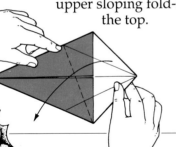

4 This should be the result. Press the paper flat.

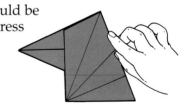

5 Turn the paper over from top to bottom. Fold the left-hand triangular point over to the right on a line between the bottom point and the upper sloping fold-line.

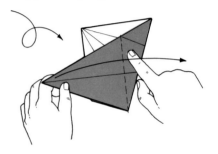

6 Fold the triangular point in half from top to bottom. While at the same time . . .

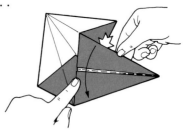

7 folding the top over to lie along the left-hand side.

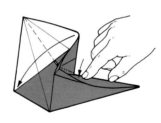

8 This shows you step 7 in more detail.

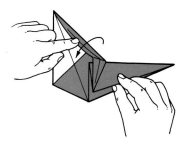

9 This should be the result. Press the paper flat, so completing one unit.

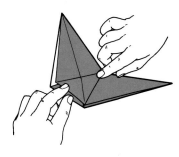

10 *Assembly:* Repeat steps 1 to 9 with the remaining three squares. Tuck one unit inside another as shown. Glue them together.

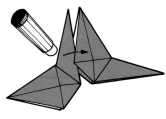

11 Keep on tucking and gluing units together carefully, until you have built up a 'flat' star.

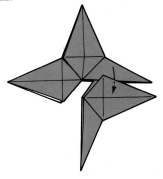

12 Turn the star over.

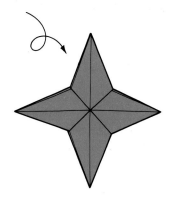

13 Carefully press each side of the star as shown by the arrows, so making it take on a three-dimensional form.

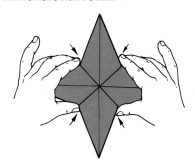

14 To complete, attach a loop of cotton to the star, so that you can hang it from the Christmas tree.

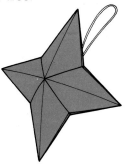

Christmas wreath

Room decoration

When wreaths are hung on the doors of our homes and shops, we know that the Christmas season has truly arrived. The following model looks very pretty when it is fixed on to a gift or displayed as a decoration.

You will need:

8 squares of paper all the same size, coloured on one side and white on the other
Ribbon decoration (page 48)
Glue
Several sticky-backed circles

1   Turn one square round so that it looks like a diamond, with the coloured side on top. Fold and unfold it in half from bottom to top.

2   From the left-hand corner, fold the top sloping side in to meet the middle fold-line.

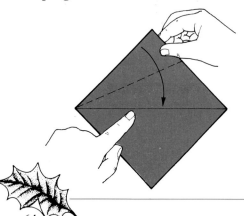

3   Fold the bottom point up along the middle fold-line, so making a triangle.

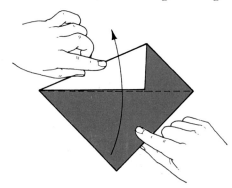

4   Fold the triangle's right-hand sloping side down to meet the bottom.

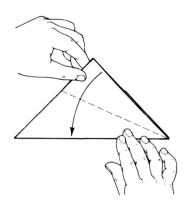

5   Fold the left-hand sloping side over to meet the vertical edge nearest to it.

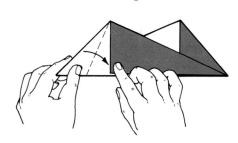

64

6   Repeat step 5 with the right-hand sloping side. Press the side flat and unfold it, so completing one unit. Repeat steps 1 to 6 with the remaining seven squares.

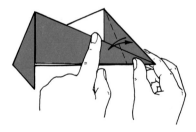

7   *Assembly:* Tuck one unit inside another as shown.

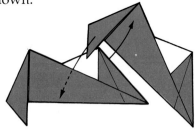

8   Along the fold-line made in step 6, fold the top unit's right-hand sloping side behind and tuck it down inside the adjoining unit, so locking them both together.

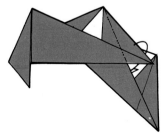

9   Repeat step 7 with another unit.

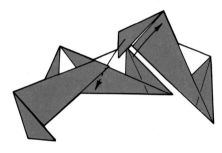

10   Repeat step 8.

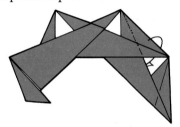

11   Keep on tucking and locking units together carefully, until you have built up the Christmas wreath.

12   To complete, glue on the ribbon decoration and decorate the wreath with sticky-backed circles.

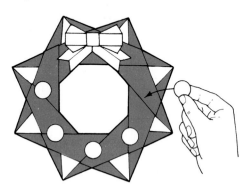

Nutcracker

Stationery/room decoration

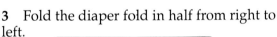

Here, from just a few basic shapes you can make a delightful figure. Why not see what other figures you can invent?

You will need:

3 squares of paper all the same size, coloured on one side and white on the other (try using a black one for the boots, a blue one for the trousers, face and hat and a red one for the tunic)
Scissors
Glue

1 From the black square cut out square A to the size shown. Repeat step 1 of the ribbon decoration on page 48 with the blue square, so making rectangles B and C.

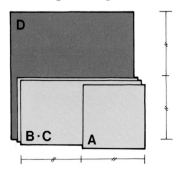

2 *Boots:* Turn the black square round so that it looks like a diamond, with the white side on top. Fold it in half from top to bottom, so making an upside-down diaper fold.

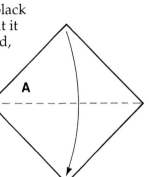

3 Fold the diaper fold in half from right to left.

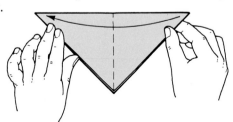

4 Turn the model round into the position as shown, so completing the boots.

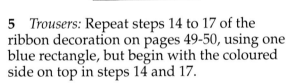

5 *Trousers:* Repeat steps 14 to 17 of the ribbon decoration on pages 49-50, using one blue rectangle, but begin with the coloured side on top in steps 14 and 17.

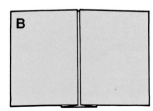

6 Turn the paper over. Fold the left-hand side in to meet the pleat's right side. Fold the right-hand side over. . .

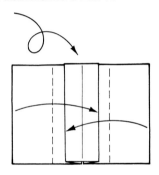

7 so that it lies on top and meets the pleat's left side. Press the paper flat.

8 Turn the paper over, so completing the trousers.

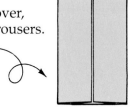

9 *Face and hat:* Place the remaining blue rectangle sideways on, with the white side on top. Fold and unfold it in half from bottom to top.

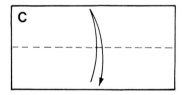

10 Fold the top and bottom right-hand corners in to meet the middle fold-line, so making a shape that looks like the roof of a house.

11 Fold the roof over along its base-line.

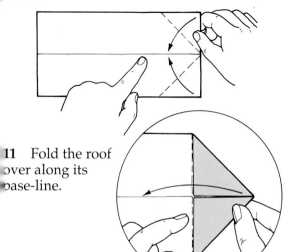

12 Fold the roof's point over to meet the right-hand side. Press the point flat and unfold it.

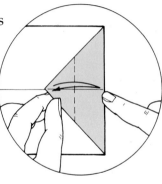

13 Fold the point over, so that the fold-line made in step 12 lies along the right-hand side.

14 Fold the point in to meet the fold-line made in step 12, so making the hat's peak.

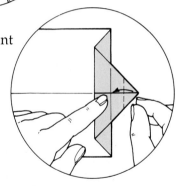

15 Fold the peak over towards the left.

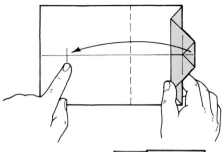

16 This should be the result. Press the paper flat.

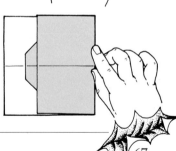

17 Turn the paper over from top to bottom. Fold the top and bottom in to meet the middle fold-line.

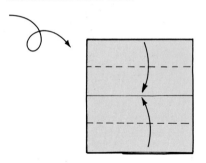

18 Fold over a little of the top and bottom left-hand corners.

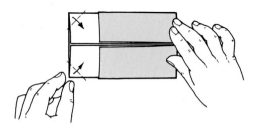

19 Turn the paper over, so completing the face and hat.

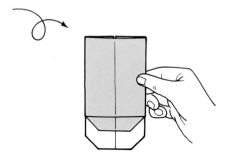

20 *Tunic:* Divide the red square into three both ways by folding, with the white side on top.

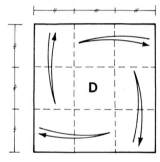

21 Fold the right-hand side over to a point one-third of the way to the opposite side.

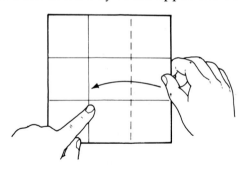

22 On the top right-hand layer of paper make the folds as shown, so . . .

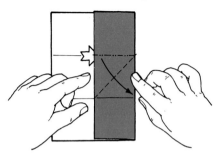

23 opening it out. Repeat steps 21 to 23 with the left-hand side.

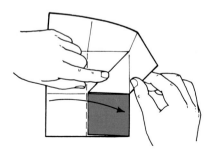

24 Flatten the opened section of paper down into the shape of a roof.

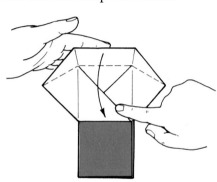

25 Fold the bottom up and tuck it underneath the roof's top layer of paper.

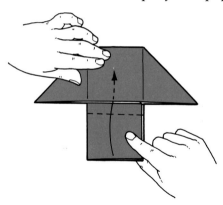

26 Fold the roof's triangular points in to meet the middle of the horizontal edge as shown.

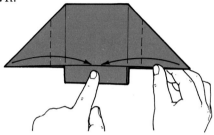

27 Fold the right-hand triangular point out along the vertical fold-line nearest to it, so making a triangle.

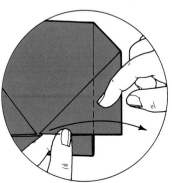

28 Open out the triangle and press it down neatly into a diamond.

29 Fold up a little of the diamond's tip.

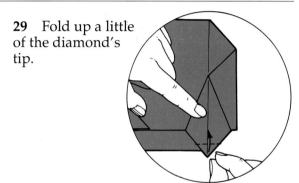

30 This should be the result. Press the paper flat. Repeat steps 27 to 30 with the left-hand triangular point.

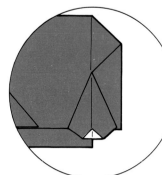

31 Turn the tunic over. *Assembly:* Glue the boots into the bottom of the trousers, the top of the trousers into the bottom of the tunic and finally the face and hat on top of the tunic as shown, so completing the Nutcracker.

Father Christmas

Stationery/room decoration

The character of Father Christmas, with his long white beard and red costume trimmed with white fur, is quite easy to fold. As always, follow the illustrations very carefully.

You will need:
4 squares of paper all the same size, coloured on one side and white on the other (try using a white one for the hands and beard, a black one for the boots and two red ones for the trousers, face, hat and tunic)
Scissors
Small white square of paper
Glue

1 From the white square cut out two squares A and one square C to the sizes shown. Also from the black square cut out square B to the size shown. Finally, repeat step 1 of the ribbon decoration on page 48 with one red square, so making rectangles D and E.

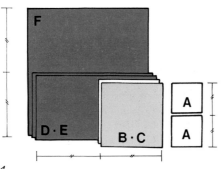

2 *Hands:* Turn one white square A round so that it looks like a diamond. Fold it in half from bottom to top, so making a diaper fold.

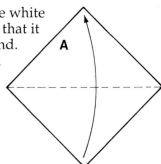

3 Fold the right-hand point over to a point one-third of the way across the diaper fold. Repeat with the left-hand point, so that it lies on top.

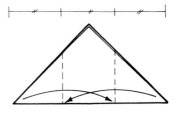

4 Fold the topmost point out to the left, into the position shown by the dotted lines, so making a thumb.

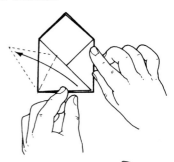

5 Fold over a little of the top point and the thumb's tip.

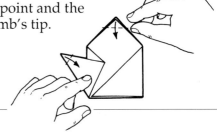

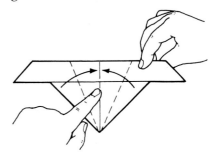

6 Turn the paper over, so making the left hand. Repeat steps 2 to 6 with the remaining square A. But in step 3 fold the left-hand point over first, then the right-hand one. And, in step 4 fold the topmost point out to the right, so making (in step 6) the right hand.

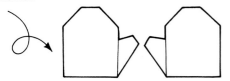

7 *Boots:* Repeat steps 2 to 4 of the Nutcracker on page 66 using the black square.

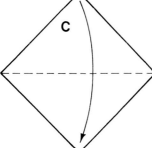

8 *Beard:* Turn the white square round so that it looks like a diamond. Fold it in half from top to bottom, so making an upside-down diaper fold.

9 Fold and unfold the diaper fold in half from right to left.

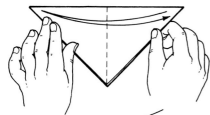

10 Fold the top down as far as shown.

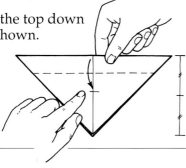

11 From the bottom point fold the lower sloping sides in to meet the middle fold-line.

12 Fold the top triangular points out as shown.

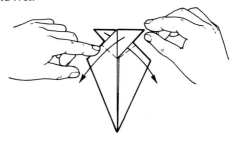

13 This should be the result. Press the paper flat, so completing the beard.

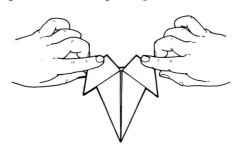

14 *Trousers:* Place one red rectangle sideways on, with the coloured side on top. Fold up a little of the bottom. Now repeat steps 14 to 17 of the ribbon decoration on pages 49-50, but begin with the coloured side on top in steps 14 and 17.

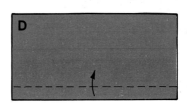

15 This should be the result. Press the paper flat.

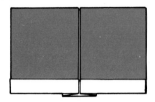

16 Turn the paper over. Fold the sides over as shown.

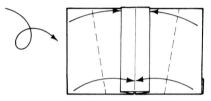

17 Turn the paper over, so completing the trousers.

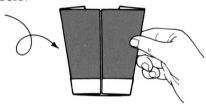

18 *Face and hat:* Place the remaining red rectangle sideways on, with the coloured side on top. Fold and unfold it in half from bottom to top. Now, fold over a little of the right-hand side.

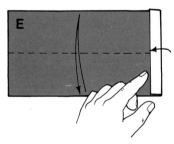

19 Turn the paper over from top to bottom. Fold the right-hand side over towards the left.

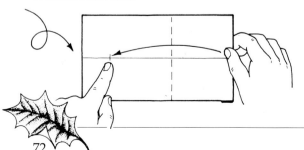

20 Turn the paper over from top to bottom. Fold the top and bottom right-hand corners in to meet the middle fold-line.

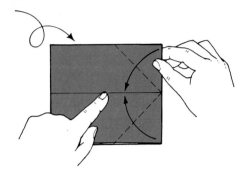

21 Fold the top and bottom in to meet the middle fold-line.

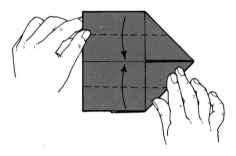

22 Fold over a little of the top and bottom left-hand corners. Fold the right-hand point over, into the position shown by the dotted lines.

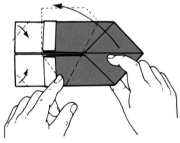

23 Turn the paper over, so completing the face and hat. Repeat steps 8 to 11 of the holly on page 16 with the small white square, so making a pompom. Glue it on to the hat's point at an attractive angle.

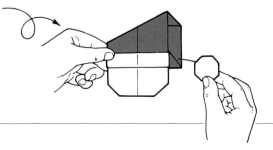

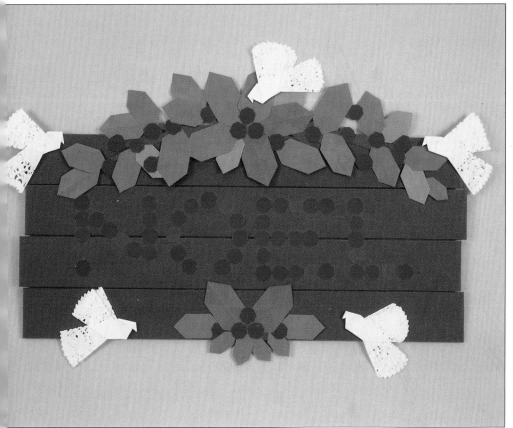

Advent calendar p107

vent calendar p107

Above:
Three-dimensional Christmas tree p77; **Reindeer** p46; **Father Christmas** p70 and **Sleigh** p90; for harnes and presentation *see* **Father Christmas and his reindeer** p110; **Christmas tree** p12; **House with a chimne** p23; **Church** p25

Left:
Gift bag p94; **Gift wrapping** p92; **Gift ta including Christmas stocking** p19; **Christm pudding** p22; **Father Christmas** p27; **Mistletoe** p17; **Ribbo decorations** p48

24 *Tunic:* Repeat steps 20 to 23 of the Nutcracker on page 68 using the remaining red square. Open it out completely.

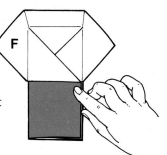

25 Turn the paper over. Fold the bottom over and over again. Fold over a little of each top corner as shown.

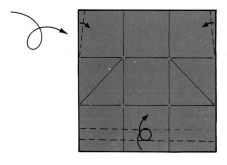

26 This should be the result. Press the paper flat.

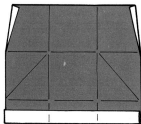

27 Turn the paper over. Refold the existing diagonal fold-lines in the lower right and left-hand squares. Then fold their lower ends over towards the bottom so that they meet each other and make the sloping fold-lines shown, and the upper section of paper rises up as in step 28.

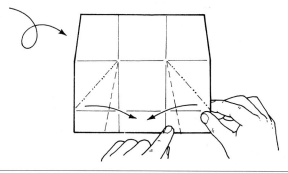

28 Flatten the upright section down neatly.

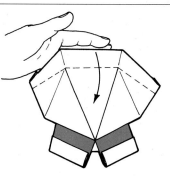

29 This should be the result. Press the paper flat, so making the tunic's sleeves.

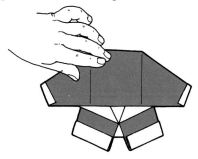

30 Turn the paper over. Fold the sleeves over as shown, so completing the tunic.

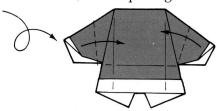

31 *Assembly:* Glue the boots into the bottom of the trousers, the top of the trousers into the bottom of the tunic, the hands into the sleeves, the face and hat on top of the tunic and finally the beard on to the face as shown, so completing Father Christmas.

Star-shaped box

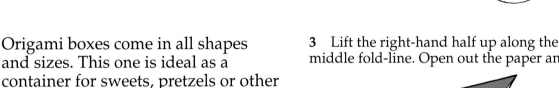

Table decoration

Origami boxes come in all shapes and sizes. This one is ideal as a container for sweets, pretzels or other party favourites.

You will need:

Square of paper, coloured on one side and white on the other

1 Turn the square round so that it looks like a diamond, with the white side on top. Fold it in half from top to bottom, so making an upside-down diaper fold.

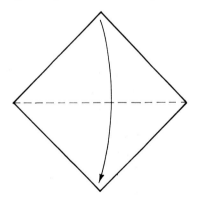

2 Fold and unfold the diaper fold in half from right to left.

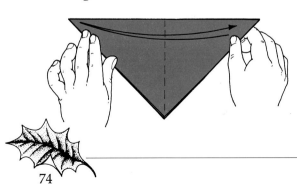

3 Lift the right-hand half up along the middle fold-line. Open out the paper and . . .

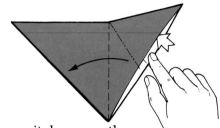

4 press it down neatly . . .

5 into a diamond.

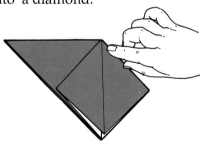

6 Turn the paper over. Repeat steps 3 to 5, so making a shape that in origami is called the preliminary fold.

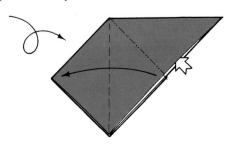

7 Fold the right and left open (unfolded) sloping sides in to meet the middle fold-line, so making two paper flaps.

8 Open out the inner edge of the right-hand flap . . .

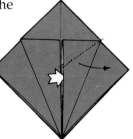

9 press it down neatly . . .

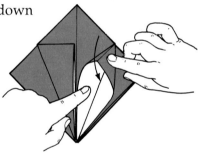

10 into a triangle. Repeat steps 8 to 10 with the left-hand flap.

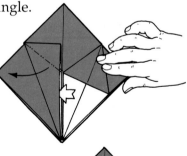

11 This should be the result. Press the paper flat.

12 Turn the paper over from side to side. Repeat steps 7 to 11.

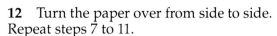
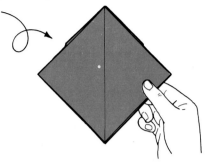

13 Fold the top right-hand section of paper over to the left, as though turning a page of a book.

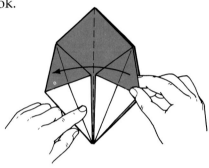

14 Fold the front flap's lower sloping sides in to meet the middle fold-line.

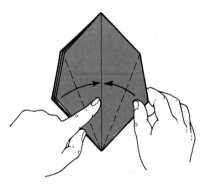

15 Fold two left-hand sections of paper over to the right, as though turning the pages of a book.

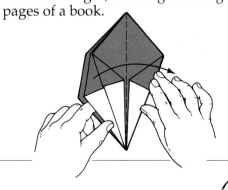

16 Repeat step 14.

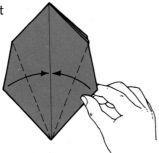

17 Fold the front point up as far as it will go.

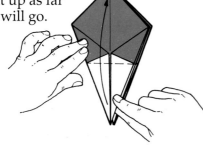

18 Repeat step 13.

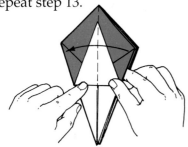

19 Repeat step 17.

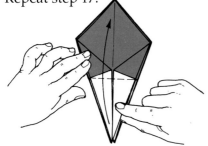

20 Repeat step 17 behind and with the remaining middle point.

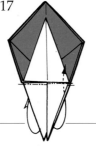

21 Turn the paper round into the position shown.

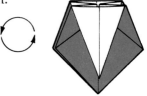

22 Pinch the front and back points and gently pull them apart, at the same time . . .

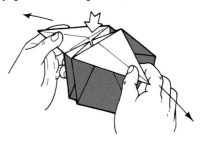

23 pushing down on the bottom point. Finally push out the square base of the box and lift up the side points.

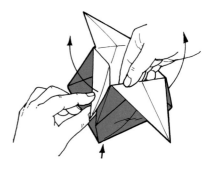

24 Here is the completed star-shaped box.

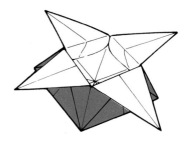

Three-dimensional Christmas tree

Stationery/room decoration

For many people the Christmas tree is the symbol of the Christmas season. So why not celebrate the beginning of the Christmas holiday by folding your own tree?

> **You will need:**
> 4 squares of paper the same size, coloured on one side and white on the other (try using three green ones for the foliage and a brown one for the trunk)
> Scissors

1 From the three green squares cut down two to the sizes shown by squares B and C, so leaving one square which is called A. Repeat step 1 of the ribbon decoration on page 48 with the brown square. Put one rectangle to one side as it is not required.

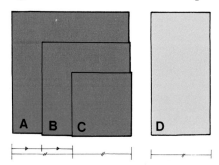

2 *Foliage:* Begin by repeating steps 1 to 6 of the star-shaped box on page 74 with square A. Tuck the front flap of paper up inside the preliminary fold, so . . .

3 folding it in half from bottom to top. Press the paper flat.

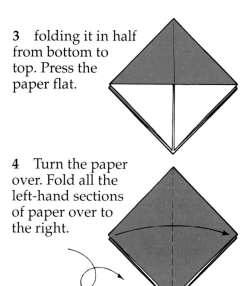

4 Turn the paper over. Fold all the left-hand sections of paper over to the right.

5 Fold all the bottom points up to meet the right-hand side point. Press the points flat and unfold them.

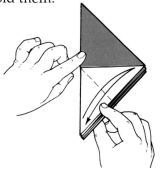

6 Fold the top right-hand section of paper over to the left, as though turning a page of a book.

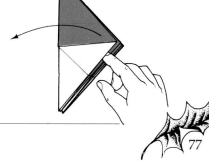

7 Fold the front flap of paper in half from bottom to top, so making a triangle.

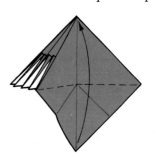

11 For the final time repeat steps 7 to 9.

8 Fold the triangle's top point over (along the existing diagonal fold-line) to meet the left-hand side point, at the same time . . .

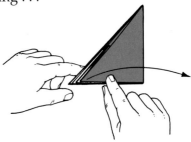

12 Open out the paper from left to right, so making . . .

9 letting the adjoining right-hand section of paper rise up. Flatten the section down and over to the left as shown.

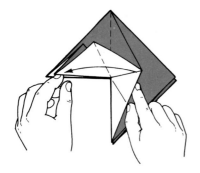

13 the foliage become three-dimensional.

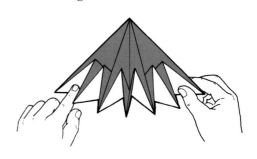

10 Repeat steps 7 to 9.

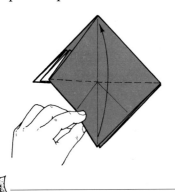

14 *Assembly:* Repeat steps 2 to 13 with squares B and C. Tuck foliage A into foliage B as shown.

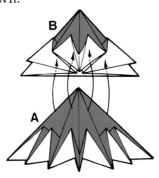

15   Finally, place foliage C on top.

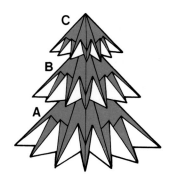

16   *Trunk:* Place the brown rectangle D sideways on, with the coloured side on top. Fold it in half from right to left.

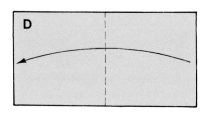

17   Again fold the paper in half from right to left.

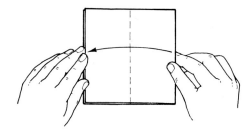

18   Repeat step 17. Press the paper flat and open it out completely.

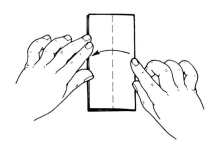

19   From the right-hand side pleat the paper backwards and forwards along the existing fold-lines, with the coloured side on top. You will have to reverse some of the fold-lines.

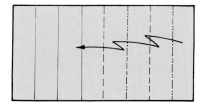

20   Fold either end pleat down, so . . .

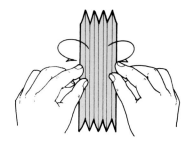

21   completing the trunk.

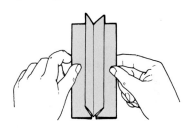

22   To complete, tuck the trunk up inside foliage A as shown. If you open out the base of the trunk a little, the tree will stand up by itself.

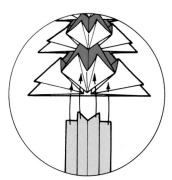

Bauble

Tree decoration

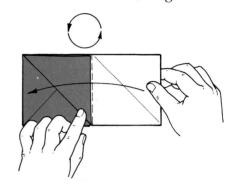

The folding of this particular model is based around a very simple unit. Even though it may appear difficult at first, the bauble can be mastered quite easily.

You will need:

6 squares of paper all the same size, coloured on one side and white on the other
Pencil
Needle and cotton

1 Begin by repeating steps 2 to 6 of the holly on pages 15-16 with each square.

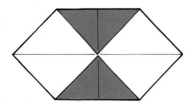

2 Turn one unit over from top to bottom. Fold it in half from top left to bottom right.

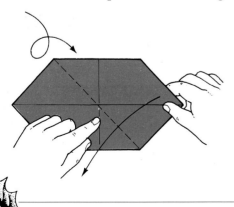

3 Turn the paper round into the position shown. Fold it in half from right to left.

4 Open out the front pocket and . . .

5 pull it over to the right.

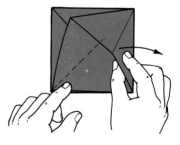

6 Press the paper down neatly as shown, so making a coloured triangular pocket and a white triangular flap.

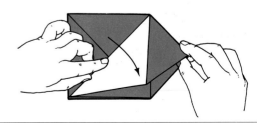

7 Turn the paper over from left to right. Fold the right-hand flap of paper over to the left. Now, repeat steps 4 to 6.

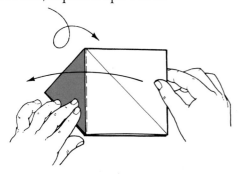

11 Tuck unit C into unit B. At the same time tuck unit A into unit C.

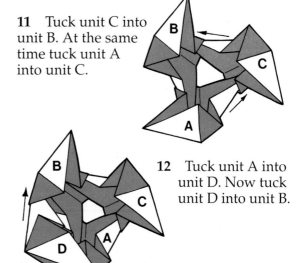

12 Tuck unit A into unit D. Now tuck unit D into unit B.

8 Fold the front pocket to point towards you and the pocket on the back to point away, so completing . . .

9 one star-like unit. Repeat steps 2 to 6 with the remaining units.

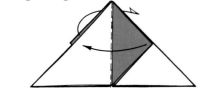

13 Tuck unit E into unit A. Carefully tuck units D and C into unit E.

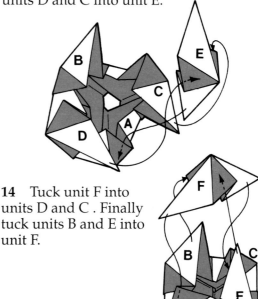

14 Tuck unit F into units D and C . Finally tuck units B and E into unit F.

10 *Assembly:* As a help during the assembly, label each unit from A to F, with the pencil. The method of joining the units together is simple: put white flaps into coloured pockets. Hold unit A between the flaps and pockets, open side up. Tuck unit B into unit A.

15 Gently push all the units snugly together. To complete the bauble, attach a loop of cotton to the top, so that it can become a hanging ornament.

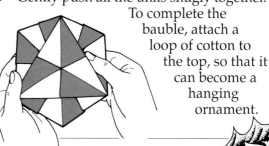

Pomander

Room decoration

Originally a pomander was an orange covered all over with cloves. It was allowed to dry slowly in a dry, warm place. The pomander then created a pleasant fragrance, the origins of which date back into history. When this origami pomander is finished it makes a wonderful decoration.

You will need:

thirty-six 15cm squares of paper, coloured on one side and white on the other
Needle and strong cotton
Scissors
40cm length of gift ribbon
20cm length of gift ribbon

1   Begin by repeating steps 1 to 6 of the star-shaped box on page 74 with one square, but with the coloured side on top in step 1. Open out the top right-hand flap of paper and . . .

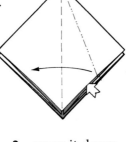

2   press it down neatly into a diamond.

3   Fold the diamond in half from left to right.

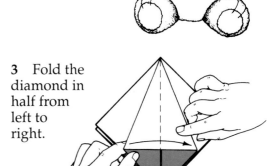

4   Repeat steps 1 and 2 with the top left-hand flap of paper.

5   Fold the diamond in half from right to left.

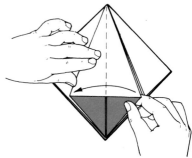

6   Turn the paper over. Repeat steps 1 to 5.

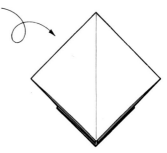

7 Fold the front flap's lower sloping sides in to meet the middle fold-line.

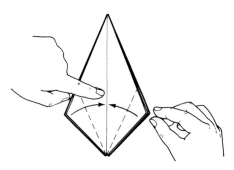

8 Fold the front point up as far as it will go.

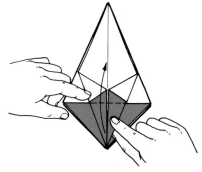

9 This should be the result. Repeat steps 7 and 8 on the three remaining flaps.

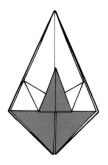

10 This should be the result. Press the paper flat. Now open it out completely.

11 Turn the paper over, so that the white side is on top. Press down on the paper's middle, so making it become bowl-like in appearance.

12 Position the paper as shown. Starting with the top point and using the existing fold-lines, take the middle of the top right and left edges behind to the middle.

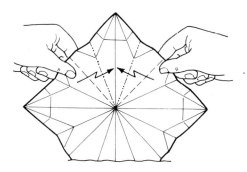

13 Fold the sloping sides in to meet the middle fold-line.

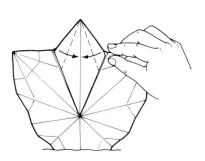

14 Fold the top point down along the line of the horizontal edge.

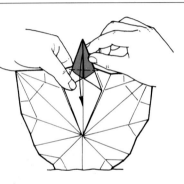

15 Take the middle of the right-hand corner's two edges behind, in effect repeating step 12. Now repeat steps 13 and 14.

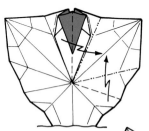

16 Repeat steps 12 to 14 with what was originally the bottom point.

17 (New position) Repeat step 12 with what was originally the left-hand corner.

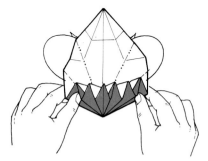

18 Repeat step 13.

19 Tuck the point down into the model, so completing one unit. Repeat steps 1 to 19 with the remaining thirty-five squares.

20 *Assembly:* Pass a length of strong cotton through the base points of nine units and . . .

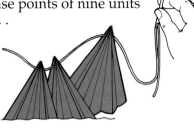

21 tie them together, so making one cluster of flowers. Now make three more such clusters.

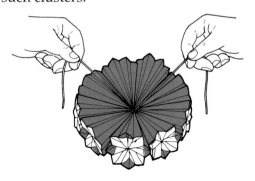

22 Cut 'V' shapes into either end of the 40cm length of ribbon. Also cut two 40cm lengths of strong cotton and place them together side by side. Lay the ribbon on the middle of the lengths of cotton.

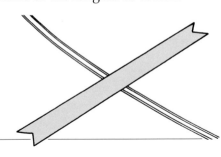

23 Tie the lengths of cotton around the ribbon's middle into a double knot. Carefully separate them into the letter 'X' as shown.

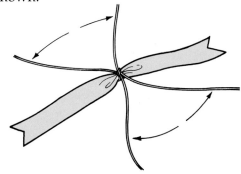

24 Place one cluster on top of the 'X'. Tie opposite lengths of cotton together into a single knot.

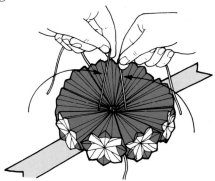

25 Tie the remaining lengths of cotton together into a single knot.

26 Place a second cluster on top. Tie opposite lengths of cotton together into a single knot. Now repeat step 25.

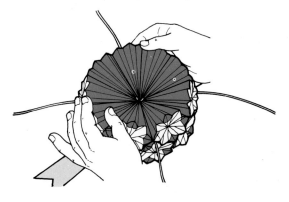

27 Repeat step 26 with the remaining two clusters. Finally hold each of two lengths of cotton together. Tie a loose knot in the centre and pull the lengths slowly. When the knot comes to the base fasten it tightly, so making the clusters become a round ball.

28 Tie the ends of the lengths of cotton into a reef knot. To complete the pomander, cut 'V' shapes into the 20cm length of ribbon and tie it into a bow around the lengths of cotton as shown.

Christmas crackers

Table decoration/party accessory

Crackers were invented by a London pastry cook call Tom Smith during the reign of Queen Victoria. If you want your cracker to bang you will have to place inside a 'snap' which you can buy from specialist suppliers of novelties.

To make one Christmas cracker you will need:

Scissors, double or metallic crepe paper, normal crepe paper, ruler, a 'snap' (to make the bang), three empty toilet rolls, glue, strong cotton, gift ribbon, motto (it may be a joke, riddle or poem), a small gift (make sure that whatever you choose will fit inside the toilet-rolls) and miniature pieces of origami

1   Cut a rectangle of double crepe paper measuring 17cm x 30cm, with the grain running lengthways. Cut a zig-zag edge in

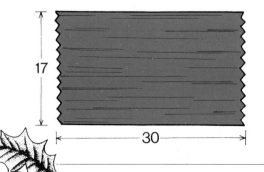

the crepe paper at both ends. Also cut a rectangle of normal crepe paper measuring 15cm x 30 cm, again making sure that the grain is running lengthways.

2   Place the rectangle of double crepe paper sideways on. Lay the snap, if you have one, across it. Turn the rectangle of normal crepe paper sideways on and position it on top of the double one, making sure that their bottom edges meet.

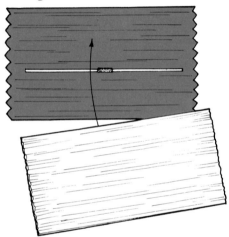

3   Lay the three toilet-rolls, end to end, along the bottom edge of the topmost rectangle of paper as shown.

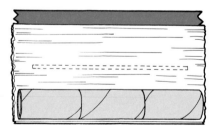

4   Glue along the top edge of the double crepe paper. Now treating them as one large tube roll up the tubes, so tightly wrapping both rectangles of paper around them.

When you get to the top, firmly stick the rolled paper to the glued edge.

5   Pull out the right-hand toilet-roll about 4cm. Lay a length of strong cotton underneath the rolled paper as shown.

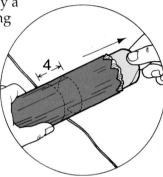

6   Bring the cotton's ends up across and pull them, at right angles to the rolls, thereby squeezing the paper and so making a neck.

7   Remove the cotton and lay a length of gift ribbon underneath the neck.

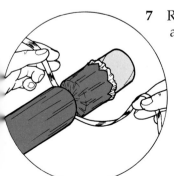

8   Tie the ribbon into a bow. Cut its ends, so making equal sized 'tails'. Finally, remove the right-hand toilet-roll.

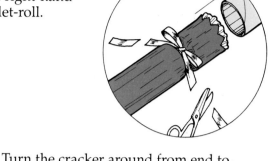

9   Turn the cracker around from end to end. Drop your motto and gift into the open end.

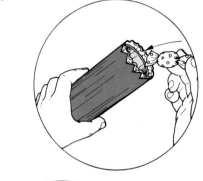

10   Now repeat steps 6 to 8.

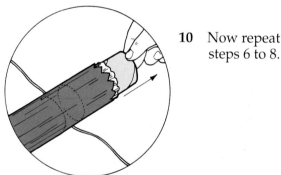

11   To complete, decorate the cracker by gluing on miniature pieces of origami.

Doily Dove

Tree/room decoration

This model makes an ideal decoration to hang from the Christmas tree or the ceiling.

You will need:
Half a paper doily
Scissors
Needle and cotton

1   Fold and unfold the doily in half from right to left, with the straight edge along the top.

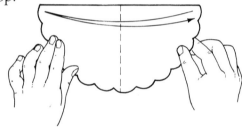

2   Fold the top corners in to meet the middle fold-line.

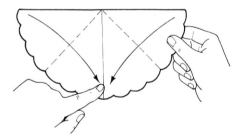

3   Fold the doily in half from right to left.

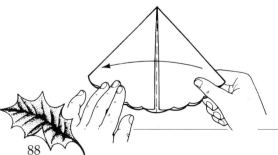

4   Turn the doily round, into the position as shown. From the middle of the doily's decorative edge, cut towards the left-hand point as far as shown, so making the dove's tail and wings.

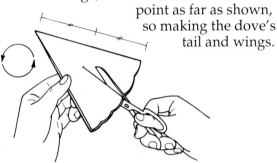

5   Fold the front wing up, into the position shown by the dotted lines. Repeat this step behind.

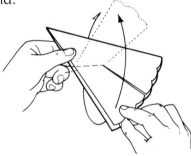

6   Repeat steps 11 to 14 of the pigeon on page 59 with the left-hand point.

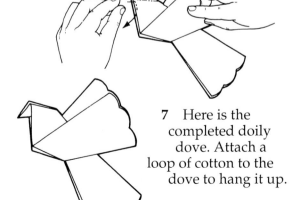

7   Here is the completed doily dove. Attach a loop of cotton to the dove to hang it up.

Garlands

Room decoration

Garlands are attractive decorations to hang on the wall or from the ceiling. They will help add that special sparkle to the Christmas season.

You will need:

Scissors
Piece of card (an old cereal carton is ideal)
Pencil
Ruler
8cm wide, long strip of craft paper
Glue

1   Cut a cardboard rectangle measuring 8cm x 10cm. Using the pencil, draw either this holly or dove design on to the rectangle as shown. Carefully cut around your pencil lines and discard the shaded parts, so making a template.

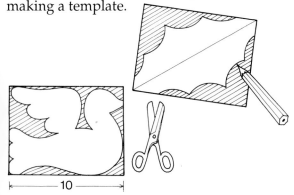

2   Place the strip of craft paper sideways on. From the right-hand end, pleat the strip in 10cm long sections, forwards and . . .

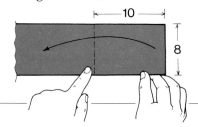

3   backwards, so making . . .

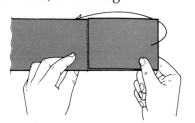

4   one long folded strip of paper, rather like a concertina.
Fold any excess paper behind, so making a joining tab.

5   Place the template on to the folded strip as shown and trace around it with the pencil.

6   Cut around the pencil outline. Be careful not to cut through the upper right-hand and lower left-hand 'folded' corners.

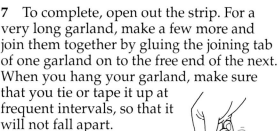

7   To complete, open out the strip. For a very long garland, make a few more and join them together by gluing the joining tab of one garland on to the free end of the next. When you hang your garland, make sure that you tie or tape it up at frequent intervals, so that it will not fall apart.

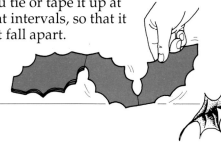

Sleigh

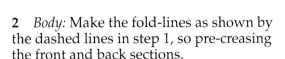

Room decoration

The sleigh when displayed with some reindeer and a Father Christmas will create that finishing touch to any seasonal scene.

You will need:
Pencil
Ruler
A 16cm x 24cm rectangle of thin moss green craft card for the sleigh
Two 3cm x 21cm rectangles of thin dark brown craft card for the runners
Scissors
Glue

1   Using the pencil and ruler, mark and measure out the sleigh's body onto the 16cm x 24cm rectangle of craft card and its two runners onto the 3cm x 21cm rectangles. Carefully cut along your pencil lines and the body's solid lines as shown. Discard the shaded parts.

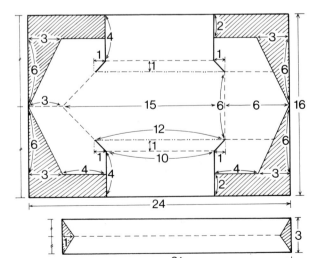

2   *Body:* Make the fold-lines as shown by the dashed lines in step 1, so pre-creasing the front and back sections.

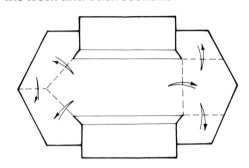

3   Pleat the top and bottom rectangles by folding them behind and forward along the fold-lines, as shown by the dashed and dotted lines in step 1, so making them become upright.

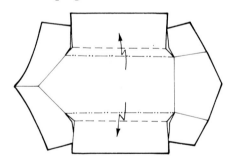

4   Along the fold-lines made in step 2 form the body's front and back sections.

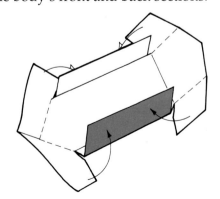

5 Glue the front and back sections to the upright rectangles, so making the body become three-dimensional.

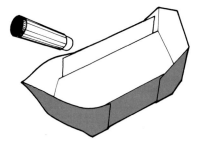

6 *Runners:* Place the runners sideways on and fold them in half from bottom to top.

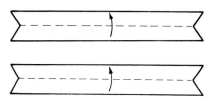

7 Fold the right-hand sloping edge of one runner over, at a point that is 3cm from the runner's bottom corner.

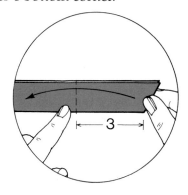

8 Fold the sloping edges up, into the position shown by the dotted lines. Press the edges flat and unfold them.

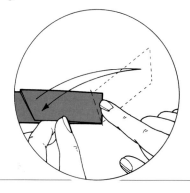

9 Along the fold-lines made in steps 7 and 8, pleat the paper on either side of the sloping edges.

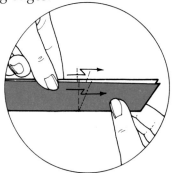

10 Glue the layers of the sloping edges together, so completing one runner. Repeat steps 7 to 10 with the remaining runner.

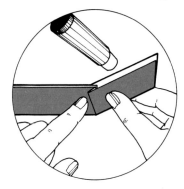

11 Glue along the body's bottom edges. Tuck the glued edges into the runners as shown. Pinch them together, so completing the sleigh. To fit this particular sized sleigh, as in the photograph on the front cover, fold reindeer from 15cm squares and a Father Christmas from 12cm ones.

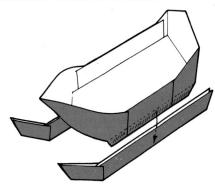

Gift wrapping

Wrapping

At Christmas-time a lot of care and thought go into gift giving. The way a gift is wrapped can say a lot about its selection. So here is an easy way to wrap and decorate a gift.

You will need:
Sheet of gift wrapping paper, coloured on one side and white on the other
A gift box
Scissors
Sticky tape
Spool of gift ribbon

1 Place the sheet of wrapping paper sideways on, with the white side on top. Turn the gift box lengthways on and place it in the middle of the paper. Fold the right-hand side up over the gift box.

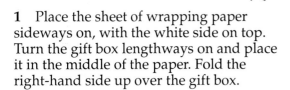

2 Fold the left-hand side up over the gift box. If the sides do not meet then you need to start again with a larger sheet of paper. If they overlap, so that the paper is impossible to handle, cut it down to a reasonable size. Hold the sides in place with the help of a piece of sticky tape.

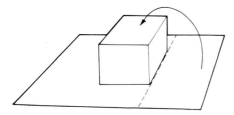

3 Push the paper down along the top of the gift box, while at the same time pressing the paper along the diagonal fold-lines as shown. Be careful to keep your folding neat and tidy.

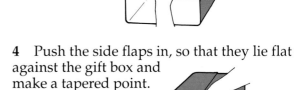

4 Push the side flaps in, so that they lie flat against the gift box and make a tapered point.

5 Fold the point over along the bottom of the gift box. Should the point protrude beyond the gift box's top edge, either fold it behind itself, or cut it off.

6 Hold the point in place with the help of a piece of sticky tape. Stand the partially wrapped gift box upright.

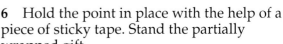
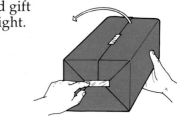

7   Repeat step 3.

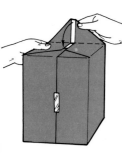

8   Repeat steps 4 and 5. Finally, hold the point in place with the help of a piece of sticky tape.

9   Unwind some ribbon from its spool. Turn the wrapped gift box lengthways on and place it on the ribbon. Bring the lengths of ribbon up around the . . .

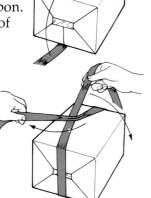

10   gift box's middle. Twist one length of ribbon around the other as shown.

11   Take the right-hand length of ribbon down underneath the gift box and bring it . . .

12   out the other side. Pass the same length of ribbon underneath the twisted section as shown.

13   Pull the lengths of ribbon apart, so tightening the twisted section.

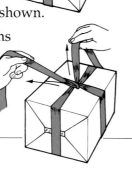

14   With the left-hand length of ribbon make a fair-sized loop. Twist the right-hand length in an anticlockwise direction around the loop you are holding, so creating a band of ribbon.

15   Push the right-hand length underneath the band of ribbon, as shown, so making . . .

16   another equal sized loop.

17   Hold the loops and pull them apart, so tightening the band of ribbon.

18   Fold the right-hand length of ribbon in half from bottom to top. At a point that is not too far from the loops, make a sloping cut into the ribbon as shown, so making a 'V' shaped 'tail'. Repeat this step with the left-hand length, so making another 'tail' which is the same length as the previous one.

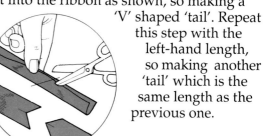

19   Here is the completed wrapped gift box.

Gift bag

Wrapping

The gift bag is very easy to make and can look very decorative. It can be made in many different sizes. Once you have learned the basic technique many variations are possible.

You will need:
Sheet of gift wrapping paper, coloured on one side and white on the other
Glue
Scissors
Gift
Ribbon bow

1 Place the sheet of wrapping paper sideways on, with the white side on top. Fold over a little of the right-hand side, so making a coloured band of paper.

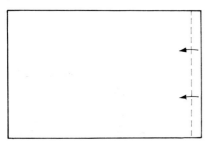

2 Apply glue to the band of paper as shown by the shaded part. Fold the paper in half from left to right and . . .

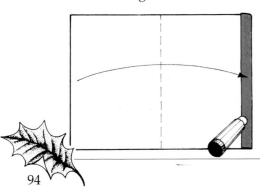

3 press firmly, so making a flat tube.

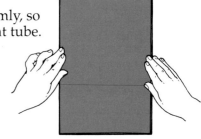

4 Turn the tube round, so that the glued section is at the top. Place your hand into the tube's right-hand side and slide it down towards you, so . . .

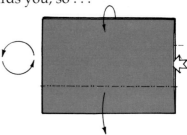

5 rolling the top layer of paper down into this position. Remove your hand from the tube. Press the tube down neatly into its new position.

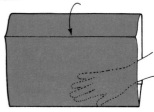

6 Fold the horizontal fold-line up to meet the top, so pleating the paper, and the bottom section of paper rise up as in step 7.

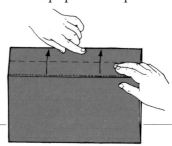

7 Fold the horizontal 'folded' edge down to meet the bottom, so pleating the paper once again.

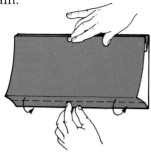

8 Fold the right-hand side over, at a point that is three times the pleat's width, so making a flap of paper.

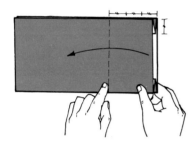

9 Fold the flap's right-hand side over to a point one-third of the way to its left-hand side. Press the side flat and unfold it.

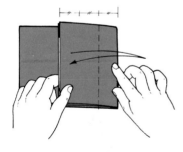

10 Stand the flap upright. Open it out, so that . . .

11 the inside layers rise up. Flatten the folded edge of each layer . . .

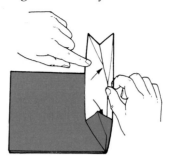

12 to form triangles, so making an open box-like shape along the fold-lines made in step 9. Collapse the box by pushing the top and bottom edges in, so that they lie flat against the triangles and make tapered points.

13 Fold the left-hand tapered point over along the vertical fold-line nearest to it.

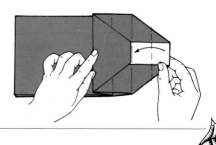

14 Fold the right-hand tapered point over to meet the vertical fold-line nearest to it.

15 Apply glue to the top of the right-hand tapered point, as shown by the shaded part. Then fold it over along the vertical fold-line nearest to it. Press firmly, so making a flat gift bag.

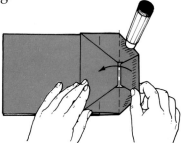

16 Turn the gift bag round, into the position as shown. Open out the bag along its top edge.

17 Place your gift inside the bag. Close the bag up.

18 From either side, make two horizontal cuts as far as shown, so making a collar.

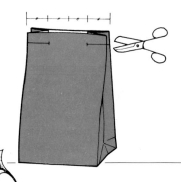

19 Fold either end of the collar over on a slant.

20 Fold the top right and left-hand corners behind on a slant. Glue the ribbon bow on to the collar.

21 Here is the completed gift bag.

CREATIVE IDEAS

Making Advent calendars, sending cards and creating beautiful scenes have become a very special part of Christmas holiday. In 'Creative Ideas' you will find suggestions on how to use and display your finished origami. It also contains advice on making the 'finishing touches' that we have included in the photographs. They are not origami, but they will help give that something special to your Christmas origami. Do remember that it is the finishing touches that make your work look attractive. By all means aim to copy the scenes exactly as they appear in the photographs but don't forget that what is important is your own personal style and how you develop the illustrated ideas.

Remember that the real secret of origami lies in the giving and sharing with others. We do hope that you have a lot of fun and enjoyment with *The Christmas Origami Book.*

Handling of tools

Always take great care when handling any sharp-edged or pointed tools, so as not to cut yourself. It is a good idea to keep them in a safe place, like a box with a lid, and out of reach of any younger members of the family.

Using a craft knife

Remember that a craft knife can be very sharp. When using one, always tell an adult what you are going to do (or ask them to help you), and always do any cutting on a piece of old board, so that you do not cut yourself or damage any surfaces.

1   Place a metal ruler next to the line to be cut and hold it down firmly, as shown. Then carefully guide the point of a craft knife along the ruler's metal edge, so cutting through your material.

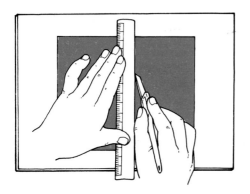

Using scissors

Remember scissors can be very sharp and use them carefully. For a sharp, clean cut always keep the scissor's blades at 90 degrees to the paper and do not twist and turn them around.

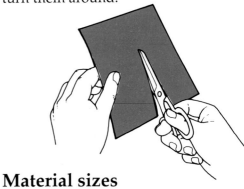

Material sizes

A word concerning materials: do remember that all the measurements and sizes given for craft materials and models in 'Creative Ideas' are approximate, and that they can be changed to fit your personal requirements. But be careful not to make objects too small, as later on you could have problems with the construction of your chosen project.

Decorative place card

Here is an attractive way to decorate a place card.

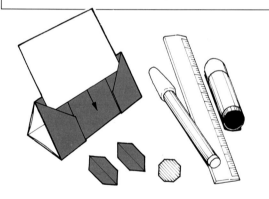

You will need:

Felt-tip pen
Ruler
Small rectangle of card that just fits inside the place card stand
Glue
Miniature holly decoration (see page 15)
Place card stand (see page 31)

1   Using the felt-tip pen and ruler, mark and measure out a border design on to the small rectangle of card, as shown.

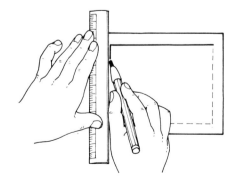

2   Glue the miniature holly decoration on to the card as shown.

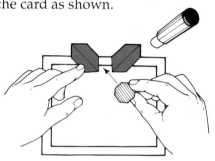

3   Using the felt-tip pen write on your guest's name. For a more attractive looking place card try using sticky-backed letters.

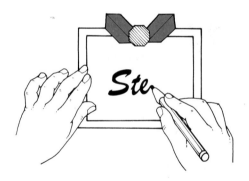

4   Finally, slip the rectangle of card in to the place card stand, behind the pleat's sloping edges, as shown.

Origami Christmas card

One of the many things that you can do with origami is to make your own Christmas cards. To make the following card projects you will need a single card. Here is a quick and easy way to make one.

You will need:
Rectangle of craft paper, about A4 in size
Glue
Miniature pieces of origami

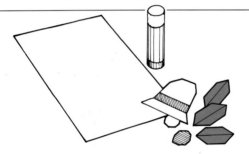

1   Place the rectangle of craft paper sideways on, and fold it in half from left to right.

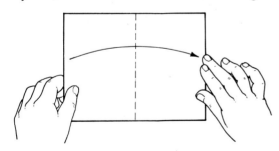

In 1846 the very first Christmas cards were created by the first director of London's Victoria and Albert Museum, Henry Cole. He had one thousand hand coloured cards produced and they could be bought at Felix Summerly's Treasure House for one shilling (five pence) each.

2   Run your forefinger along the left-hand side to both edges, pressing the fold in place, so completing the single card.

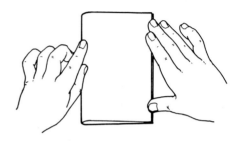

3   Decorate the front of the card by gluing on the miniature pieces of origami.

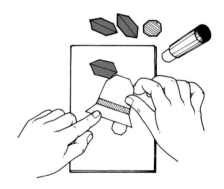

4   Here is the completed origami Christmas card. For more ideas, look at the photo section.

Window card

Do try to make this design accurately, otherwise the finished Christmas card will not look neat and tidy.

You will need:

Pencil
Small rectangle of white craft paper
Scissors
Single card (see page 100)
Glue
Craft knife
Felt-tip pen
Church folded from a square 15cm in size (see page 25)
A few miniature Christmas trees (see page 12)
Small white sticky-backed circles

1 Using the pencil, mark out a window design on to the small rectangle of white craft paper, as shown. Carefully cut around your pencil line and discard the shaded part.

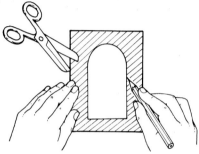

2 Open out the single card completely. Apply glue on to the back of the window and attach it on to the right-hand half of the card. Allow the glue to dry.

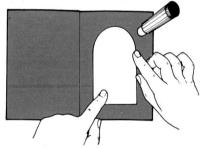

3 Using the pencil, mark out a frame design on to the window, as shown. Carefully cut around your pencil lines and discard the shaded parts.

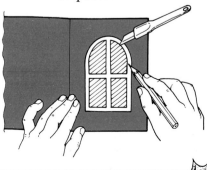

4 Turn the card over from right to left. Using the felt-tip pen, mark the horizon and colour in the sky on the right-hand half of the card, as shown.

5 Apply glue on to the back of the church and a miniature Christmas tree and attach them on to the horizon. Decorate the foreground by gluing on the remaining trees.

6 To suggest snowflakes, stick on to the scene a few sticky-backed circles, as shown.

7 Close the card in half from left to right, so completing . . .

8 the window card.

Pop-up cards

The following designs show you how to create a simple three-dimensional effect that will pop-up when the card is opened. A single card is required for each pop-up.

> **You will need:**
>
> Reindeer folded from a square 15cm in size (see page 46)
> Glue
> Single card (see page 100)
> Miniature hearts (see page 53)
> Small white sticky-backed circles
> Three-dimensional Christmas tree folded from squares 15cm in size (see page 77)
> Miniature stars (see page 9)

1 *Reindeer pop-up card:* Unfold the bottom points from inside the reindeer on a line between the bottom of the tail and the bottom of the neck.

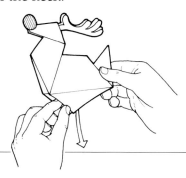

2 Apply glue on to the reindeer's topmost bottom point, as shown by the shaded part.

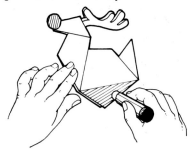

3 Open out the single card completely. Turn the reindeer over from the left to right and attach it on to the right-hand half of the card, as shown. Make sure that the reindeer's bottom edge is positioned next to the card's middle fold-line.

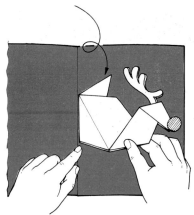

4 Repeat step 2.

5 Close the card in half from left to right and . . .

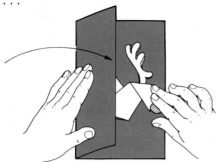

6 press firmly.

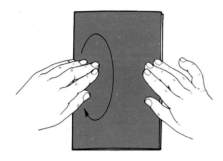

7 Open the card. The reindeer will pop-up. Finally, decorate around the reindeer by gluing on to the card the miniature hearts and a few sticky-backed circles, as shown.

8 *Three-dimensional Christmas tree pop-up card:* Open out the single card completely. Apply glue onto the back of the Christmas tree and attach it on to the card, along the middle fold-line, as shown by the shaded part.

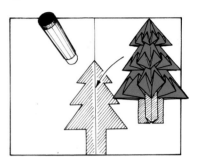

9 Repeat steps 5 and 6. Open out the card. The Christmas tree will pop-up. Finally, decorate around the tree by gluing on to the card the miniature stars and a few sticky-backed circles, as shown.

It was Prince Albert, the husband of Queen Victoria, who made the Christmas tree popular in England. He was born in Germany, where a decorative tree was already part of the Christmas festivities. Prince Albert introduced a Christmas tree into the royal household in 1840, and very soon many other people copied him.

Noel display

Christmas decorations do not have to be complicated to look pretty. Origami display are fun to hang throughout the house, and they make an enchanting addition to the Christmas season.

You will need:

Rectangle of brown craft card
Felt-tip pen
Ruler
Craft knife
Pencil
Glue
A large quantity of miniature holly berries (see page 15)
Holly leaves in a variety of different sizes (see page 15)
A few doily doves (see page 88)

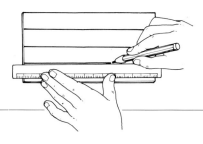

1   Place the rectangle of brown craft card sideways on. Using the felt-tip pen and ruler, mark and measure out four equal sized rectangles on to the card, as shown.

2   Using the craft knife, carefully cut away and discard the shaded parts as shown, so suggesting four staggered panels.

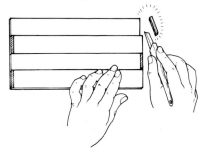

3   Using the pencil, lightly write the word 'NOEL' on to the middle two panels, as shown.

4   Apply glue on to the back of a few berries and carefully attach them on to the letters. Carry on repeating this step until all the letters are covered and form the word 'NOEL'.

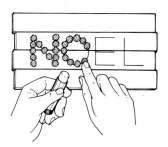

5 Decorate the top and bottom of the display by gluing on an attractive arrangement of holly leaves.

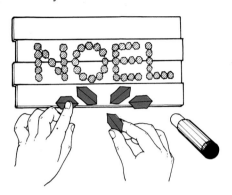

6 Repeat step 5 with any remaining holly berries.

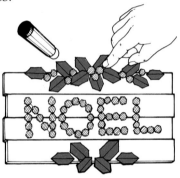

7 Finally, glue the doily doves on to the display.

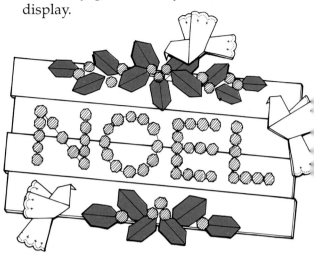

The word Noel in English, means a Christmas carol, or the shout of joy in a carol. It is also French for Christmas day.

Advent calendar

Another type of Christmas decoration is the advent calendar. Why not make one for a younger brother or sister? In step 8 try using sticky-backed numbers for a more attractive looking calendar.

You will need:
2 A1 rectangles of craft card
Craft knife
Metal ruler
Pencil
Felt-tip pen
Glue
24 origami models folded from squares less than 8cm in size
2 ribbon decorations folded from squares 15cm in size (see page 48)
Miniature holly berries and leaves (see page 15)

1 Place one A1 rectangle of craft card sideways on. Using the craft knife and metal ruler, carefully cut it in half, so making rectangles A and B.

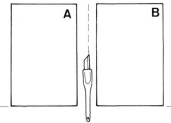

2 *Rectangle A:* Using the pencil and metal ruler, mark and measure out 12 equal sized windows on to rectangle A, as shown. Make sure that you leave spaces between each window and the card's sides and edges.

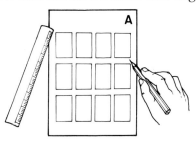

3 Using the felt-tip pen and metal ruler, go over your pencil lines, so reinforcing them.

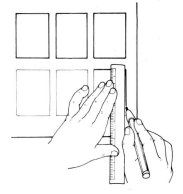

4 Using the craft knife and metal ruler, carefully cut along one window's short sides, and its right-hand side, shown by the dotted lines. Repeat this step with the remaining eleven windows.

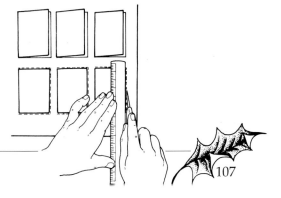

5   Open out each window along its left-hand side.

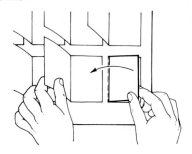

6   Apply glue all over the back of rectangle A (but not on the windows), and attach it to rectangle B. Press down firmly.

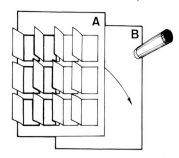

7   Glue an origami model behind each window.

8   Close each window. Using the felt-tip pen, and starting with the upper left-hand window, number them from 1 through to 12, so completing one section of the Advent calendar.

9   Repeat steps 1 to 8 with the remaining A1 rectangle of craft card. But in step 8 number the windows from 13 through to 24.

10   Finally, decorate around the sides and edges of each section by gluing on miniature holly berries and leaves and a ribbon decoration, as shown.

The advent calendar was originally a German custom. The very first Advent calendars were pictures which had twenty four windows cut in them, and behind each window there was a sweet or small gift. Present day Advent calendars have pictures behind each window, and the last one is always opened on Christmas Eve. Remember that Advent (which means 'coming') starts on 1 December, so from then onwards open a window every day to find an origami model of a star, snowman or other Christmas symbol.

Frosty drinking glass

This can be fun to make and it will bring plenty of oohs and ahs from your friends. It might be a good idea, though, to ask an adult's permission before you raid the cupboards. If you take all the eggs and sugar you might find yourself doing without breakfast!

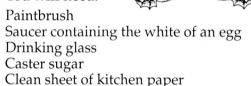

You will need:

Paintbrush
Saucer containing the white of an egg
Drinking glass
Caster sugar
Clean sheet of kitchen paper

1   Dip the paintbrush into the saucer of egg white and then carefully paint on to the drinking glass an attractive design.

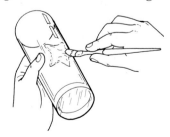

2   Pour some caster sugar on to the sheet of kitchen paper. Being very careful not to let the egg white run, gently roll the glass in

the sugar. The sugar will stick to the area which you have painted.

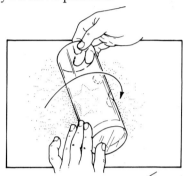

3   Dip the rim of the glass into the egg white.

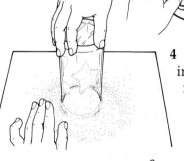

4   Dip the rim into the sugar. Stand the glass upright and allow it to dry before you use it.

5   Finally, pour a drink into the glass, so making your design show up. Why not use a windmill gift tag (see page 54) as a drinks mat?

Father Christmas and his reindeer

This display will bring that very special Christmas magic to your festive celebrations. For the correct sizes of paper for the models look back at step 11 of the sleigh on page 91.

You will need:

Pencil
Ruler
Scissors
Rectangle of craft paper, about A4 in size
Glue
1 Rudolf reindeer (see page 47, step 15)
4 reindeer (see page 46)
Long length of colourful string
Sleigh (see page 90)
Sticky tape
Father Christmas (see page 70)
A few small gifts or sweets to fit in to the sleigh

1 *Reindeer's harness:* Using the pencil and ruler, mark and measure out these four rectangles on to the craft paper. Carefully cut them out. Do not discard the excess paper. As a help during the assembly of the harness, lightly label each rectangle from A to C, with the pencil, as shown.

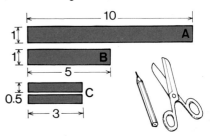

2 *Rectangles C:* Bend one rectangle C into a loop, so that the ends meet. Glue the ends together. Repeat this step with the remaining rectangle C.

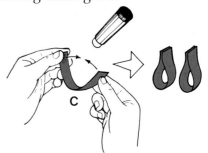

3 *Rectangle A:* Apply glue on to the back of the loops C and attach one to either end of rectangle A, as shown by the shaded part.

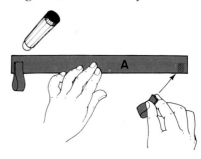

110

4 Bend rectangle A into a loop, so that loops C are on the inside.

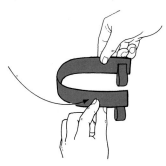

5 Open out Rudolf slightly. Apply glue on to the inside of loop A and attach it either side Rudolf's body, as shown by the shaded part. Be careful . . .

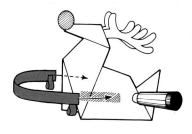

6 not to press Rudolf and loops A and C flat, but to keep them three-dimensional.

7 *Rectangle B:* Bend rectangle B into a loop. Apply glue to inside of loop B and attach it either side Rudolf's body, as shown by the shaded part. Allow the glue to dry.

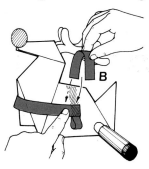

8 Here is the completed harness. Repeat steps 1 to 7 with the remaining four reindeer.

9 *Reins:* Loop the length of colourful string in half and pass the ends through loops C that are on either side Rudolf's body, as shown.

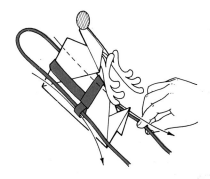

10 Passing the ends of the string through each reindeers's left-hand harness loop, attach them on to the reins, as shown. Be careful not to bunch the reindeer together.

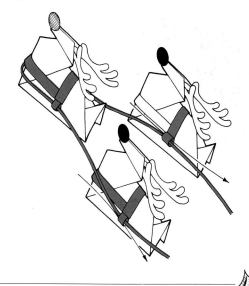

11   Cut the string at a point that is about 15cm from the end reindeer. Place the excess lengths of string to one side.

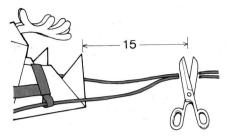

12   Tie the ends of the reins together, into a knot and fasten them on to the bottom of the sleigh with a piece of sticky tape, as shown.

13   Finally, place Father Christmas and your small gifts or sweets in the sleigh.

14   Here is the completed display of Father Christmas coming from the North Pole in a sleigh pulled by his famous reindeer.

Father Christmas has his origins in Christian and Pagan traditions. The Christian origins have come from the 4th century saint called Nicholas, who was also the Archbishop of Lycia. The Pagan origins go back to Roman and Norse people. The Norsemen thought that their god Woden brought them presents during his mid-winter celebrations.

The present day figure of Father Christmas has its origins in America. Thomas Nast, an American, produced a drawing of Father Christmas for Harpers magazine in the 1860's. It showed him as a happy old man with a long white beard and wearing a red costume trimmed with white fur.

In 1832 Clement Clarke Moore wrote a poem called 'A visit from St. Nicholas' and from this poem the reindeer become part of the ever growing Christmas tradition. Clement gave the reindeer their names of Dasher, Dancer, Prancer, Vixen, Comet, Cupid, Donner, and Blitzen. The ever popular Rudolf made his first appearance in 1939, when a song was him and his glowing red